The Lesser Key of Solomon
Aleister Crowley
S. L. MacGregor Mathers

KING SOLOMON
© 2020 ENTREACACIAS, S.L.
ENTREACACIAS, SL
[Publishing House]
Palacio Valdés, 3-5, 1ºC
33002 Oviedo - Asturias (Spain)
First edition: February, 2021

The Lesser Key of
Solomon

GOETIΛ

CONTAINS ALMOST TWO HUNDRED DIAGRAMS AND SEALS FOR INVOCATION AND
CONVOCATION OF SPIRITS. NECROMANCY, WITCHCRAFT AND BLACK ART. TRANSLATED
FROM ANCIENT MANUSCRIPTS IN THE BRITISH MUSEUM, LONDON

by
S.L. MacGregor Mathers
And
Aleister Crowley

[1904]

KING SOLOMON

Preface

This translation of the FIRST BOOK of the "*Lemegeton*" which is now for the first time made accessible to students of TALISMANIC MAGIC was done, after careful collation and edition, from numerous *Ancient Manuscripts* in *Hebrew, Latin*, and *French*, by G. H. Fra. D.D.C.F., by the order of the *Secret Chief* of the *Rosicrucian Order.*[1] The G. H. Fra., having succumbed unhappily to the assaults of the *Four Great Princes* (acting notably under Martial influences), it seemed expedient that the work should be brought to its conclusion by another hand. The investigation of a competent Skryer into the house of our unhappy *Fra.*, confirmed this divination; neither our *Fra.* nor his *Hermetic Mul.* were there seen; but only the terrible shapes of the evil *Adepts* S.V.A.[2] and H., whose original bodies having been sequestered by Justice, were no longer of use to them. On this we stayed no longer Our Hand; but withdrawing Ourselves, and

---

[1] Mr. A. E. Waite writes ("Real History Of The Rosicrucians," p. 426): "I beg leave to warn my readers that all persons who proclaim themselves to be Rosicrucians are simply members of pseudo-fraternities, and that there is that difference between their assertion and the fact of the case in which the essence of a lie consists!" It is within the *Editor's* personal knowledge that Mr. Waite was (and still is probably) a member of a society claiming to be the R.C. fraternity As *Mr. Waite* constantly hints in his writing that he is in touch with initiated centres, I think the *syllogism*, whose premises are given above, is fair, if not quite formal.~ED.

[2] It was owing to our *Fra.* receiving this S.V.A. as his Superior, and giving up the *Arcana* of our *Fraternity* into so unhallowed a power, that We decided no longer to leave Our dignity and authority in the hands of one who could be thus easily imposed upon. (For by a childish and easy magical trick did S.V.A. persuade D.D.C.F. of that lie.)

consulting the Rota, and the Books M. and Q. did decide to ask Mr. Aleister Crowley, a poet, and skilled student of *Magical Lore*, and an expert *Kabbalist*, to complete openly that which had been begun in secret.[3] This is that which is written: "His Bishoprick let another take." And again: "*Oculi Tetragammaton.*" This is also that which is said: "Nomen Secundum refertur ad *Gebhurah*; qui est Rex *Bittul* atque Corruptio *Achurajim Patris et Matris* hoc indigitatur."

And so saying we wish you well.

Ex Deo Nascimur.

In Jesu Morimur.

Per S.S. Reviviscimus.

Given forth from our Mountain of A., this day of C.C. 1903 A. D.

---

[3] He that is appointed to complete in secret that which had been begun openly is R.R., and to be heard of at the care of the Editor.

Preliminary Invocation.

Thee I invoke, the Bornless one.

Thee that didst create the Earth and the Heavens:

Thee that didst create the Night and the Day.

Thee that didst create the Darkness and the Light.

Thou art Osorronophris: Whom no man has seen at any time.

Thou art Jäbas.

Thou art Jäpôs:

Thou hast distinguished between the Just and the Unjust.

Thou didst make the Female and the Male.

Thou didst produce the Seed and the Fruit.

Thou didst form Men to love one another, and to hate one another.

I am Mosheh Thy Prophet, unto Whom Thou didst commit Thy Mysteries, the Ceremonies of Ishrael:

Thou didst produce the moist and the, dry, and that which nourisheth all created Life.

Hear Thou Me, for I am the Angel of Paphrô Osorronophris: this is Thy True Name, handed down to the Prophets of Ishrael.

****

Hear Me:~

Ar: Thiao: Rheibet: Atheleberseth:

A: Blatha: Abeu: Ebeu: Phi:

Thitasoe: Ib: Thiao.

Hear Me, and make all Spirits subject unto Me: so that every Spirit of the Firmament and of the Ether; upon the Earth and under the Earth: on dry Land and in the Water: of Whirling Air, and of rushing Fire: and every Spell and Scourge of God may be obedient unto Me.

****

I invoke Thee, the Terrible and Invisible God: Who dwellest in the Void Place of the Spirit:~

Arogogorobraô: Sothou:

Modoriô: Phalarthaô: Döö: Apé, The Bornless One:

Hear Me: etc.

Hear me:~

Roubriaô: Mariôdam: Balbnabaoth: Assalonai: Aphniaô: I: Thoteth: Abrasar: Aëôôü: Ischure, Mighty and Bornless One!

Hear me: etc.

I invoke thee:~

Ma: Barraiô: Jôêl: Kotha:

Athorêbalô: Abraoth:

Hear Me: etc.

Hear me!

Aôth: Abaôth: Basum: Isak:

Sabaoth: Iao:

This is the Lord of the Gods:

This is the Lord of the Universe:

This is He Whom the Winds fear.

This is He, Who having made Voice by His Commandment, is Lord of All Things; King, Ruler and Helper.

Hear Me, etc.

Hear Me:~

Ieou: Pûr: Iou: Pûr: Iaôt: Iaeô: Ioou: Abrasar: Sabriam: Do: Uu: Adonaie: Ede: Edu: Angelos ton Theon: Aniaia Lai: Gaia: Ape: Diathanna Thorun.

I am He! the Bornless Spirit! having sight in the feet: Strong, and the Immortal Fire!

I am He! the Truth!

I am He! Who hate that evil should be wrought in the, World!

I am He, that lighteneth and thundereth.

I am He, from Whom is the Shower of the Life of Earth:

I am He, Whose mouth ever flameth:

I am He, the Begetter and Manifester unto the Light:

I am He; the Grace of the World:

"The Heart Girt with a Serpent" is My Name!

Come Thou forth, and follow Me: and make all Spirits subject unto Me so that every Spirit of the Firmament, and of the Ether: upon the Earth and under the Earth: on dry Land, or in the Water: of whirling Air or of rushing Fire: and every Spell and Scourge of God, may be obedient unto Me!

Iao: Sabao:

Such are the Words!

Goetia

The Lesser Key Of
Solomon

The Initiated Interpretation Of Ceremonial Magic

It is loftily amusing to the student of *Magical* literature who is not quite a fool--and rare is such a combination!--to note the criticism directed by the Philistine against the citadel of his science. Truly, since our childhood has ingrained into us not only literal belief in the Bible, but also substantial belief in *Alf Laylah* wa *Laylah*, and only adolescence can cure us, we are only too liable, in the rush and energy of dawning manhood, to overturn roughly and rashly both these classics, to regard them both on the same level, as interesting documents from the standpoint of folk-lore and anthropology, and as nothing more.

Even when we learn that the Bible, by a profound and minute study of the text, may be forced to yield up *Qabalistic* arcana of cosmic scope and importance, we are too often slow to apply a similar restorative to the companion volume, even if we are the luck holders of Burton's veritable edition.

To me, then, it remains to raise the *Alf Laylah* wa Laylah into its proper place once more.

I am not concerned to deny the objective reality of all "*magical*" phenomena; if they are illusions, they are at least as real as many unquestioned facts of daily life; and, if we follow Herbert Spencer, they are at least evidence of some cause.[4]

Now, this fact is our base. What is the cause of my illusion of seeing a spirit in the triangle of Art?

Every smatterer, every expert in psychology, will answer: "That cause lies in your brain."

---

[4] This, incidentally, is perhaps the greatest argument we possess, pushed to its extreme, against the Advaitist theories.

English children (*pace* the Education Act) are taught that the Universe lies in infinite Space; Hindu children, in the Akasa, which is the same thing.

Those Europeans who go a little deeper learn from Fichte, that the phenomenal Universe is the creation of the Ego; Hindus, or Europeans studying under Hindu Gurus, are told, that by Akasa is meant the Chitakasa. The Chitakasa is situated in the "Third Eye," *i.e.*, in the brain. By assuming higher dimensions of space, we can assimilate this fact to Realism; but we have no need to take so much trouble.

This being true for the ordinary Universe, that all sense-impressions are dependent on changes in the brain,[5] we must include illusions, which are after all sense-impressions as much as "realities" are, in the class of "phenomena dependent on brain-changes."

Magical phenomena, however, come under a special sub-class, since they are willed, and their cause is the series of "real" phenomena, called the operations of ceremonial Magic.

These consist of

(1) Sight.

The circle, square, triangle, vessels, lamps, robes, implements, etc.

(2) Sound.

The invocations.

(3) Smell.

The perfumes.

(4) Taste.

The Sacraments.

(5) Touch.

---

[5] Thought is a secretion of the brain (Weissmann). Consciousness is a function of the brain (Huxley).

As under (1).

(6) Mind.

The combination of all these and reflection on their significance.

These unusual impressions (1-5) produce unusual brain-changes; hence their summary (6) is of unusual kind. Its projection back into the apparently phenomenal world is therefore unusual.

Herein then consists the reality of the operations and effects of ceremonial magic,[6] and I conceive that the apology is ample, as far as the "effects" refer only to those phenomena which appear to the magician himself, the appearance of the spirit, his conversation, possible shocks from imprudence, and so on, even to ecstasy on the one hand, and death or madness on the other.

But can any of the effects described in this our book Goetia be obtained, and if so, can you give a rational explanation of the circumstances? Say you so?

I can, and will.

The spirits of the Goetia are portions of the human brain.

Their seals therefore represent (Mr. Spencer's projected cube) methods of stimulating or regulating those particular spots (through the eye).

The names of God are vibrations calculated to establish:

(a) General control of the brain., (Establishment of functions relative to the subtle world.)

(b) Control over the brain in detail. (Rank or type of the Spirit.)

(c) Control of one special portion. (Name of the Spirit.)

The perfumes aid this through smell. Usually the perfume will only tend to control a large area; but there is an attribution of perfumes to letters of the alphabet enabling one, by a Qabalistic formula, to spell out the Spirit's name.

_____

[6] Apart from its value in obtaining one-pointedness.

I need not enter into more particular discussion of these points; the intelligent reader can easily fill in what is lacking.

If, then, I say, with Solomon:

"The Spirit Cimieries teaches logic," what I mean is:

"Those portions of my brain which subserve the logical faculty may be stimulated and developed by following out the processes called 'The Invocation of Cimieries.'"

And this is a purely materialistic rational statement; it is independent of any objective hierarchy at all. Philosophy has nothing to say; and Science can only suspend judgment, pending a proper and methodical investigation of the facts alleged.

Unfortunately, we cannot stop there. Solomon promises us that we can (1) obtain information; (2) destroy our enemies; (3) understand the voices of nature; (4) obtain treasure; (5) heal diseases, etc. I have taken these five powers at random; considerations of space forbid me to explain all.

(1) Brings up facts from sub-consciousness.

(2) Here we come to an interesting fact. It is curious to note the contrast between the noble means and the apparently vile ends of magical rituals. The latter are disguises for sublime truths. "To destroy our enemies" is to realize the illusion of duality, to excite compassion.

(Ah! Mr. Waite, the world of Magic is a mirror, wherein who sees muck is muck.)

(3) A careful naturalist will understand much from the voices of the animals he has studied long. Even a child knows the difference of a cat's miauling and purring. The faculty may be greatly developed.

(4) Business capacity may be stimulated.

(5) Abnormal states of the body may be corrected, and the involved tissues brought back to tone, in obedience to currents started from the brain.

So for all other phenomena. There is no effect which is truly and necessarily miraculous.

Our Ceremonial Magic fines down, then, to a series of minute, though of course empirical, physiological experiments, and whoso, will carry them through intelligently need not fear the result.

I have all the health, and treasure, and logic, I need; I have no time to waste. "There is a lion in the way." For me these practices are useless; but for the benefit of others less fortunate I give them to the world, together with this explanation of, and apology for, them.

I trust that the explanation will enable many students who have hitherto, by a puerile objectivity in their view of the question, obtained no results, to succeed; that the apology may impress upon our scornful men of science that the study of the bacillus should give place to that of the baculum, the little to the great--how great one only realizes when one identifies the wand with the Mahalin-gam, up which Brahma flew at the rate of 84,000 yojanas a second for 84,000 mahakalpas, down which Vishnu flew at the rate of 84,000 croces of yojanas a second for 84,000 crores of mahakalpas--yet neither reached an end.

But I reach an end.

Boleskine House,
Foyers, N.B.

Preliminary Definition Of Magic

Lemegeton Vel Clavicula Salomonis Regis

MAGIC is the Highest, most Absolute, and most Divine Knowledge of Natural Philosophy,[7] advanced in its works and wonderful operations by a right understanding of the inward and occult virtue of things; so that true Agents[8] being applied to proper Patients,[9] strange and admirable effects will thereby be produced. Whence magicians are profound and diligent searchers into Nature; they, because of their skill, know how to anticipate an effort,[10] the which to the vulgar shall seem to be a miracle.

Origen saith that the Magical Art doth not contain anything subsisting, but although it should, yet that it must not be Evil, or subject to contempt or scorn; and doth distinguish the *Natural Magic* from that which is *Diabolical.*

Apollonius Tyannaeus only exercised the *Natural Magic,* by the which he did perform wonderful things.

Philo Hebraeus saith that true Magic, by which we do arrive at the understanding of the Secret Works of Nature, is so far from being contemptible that the greatest Monarchs and Kings have studied it.

---

[7] This Preliminary Definition of Magic is found in very few Codices, and is probably later than the body of the work.
[8] Or Actives.
[9] Or Passives.
[10] Or Effect.

Nay! among the Persians none might reign unless he was skilful in this GREAT ART.

This Noble Science often degenerateth, from *Natural* becometh *Diabolical*, and from *True Philosophy* turneth unto *Nigromancy*.[11] The which is wholly to be charged upon its followers, who, abusing or not being capable of that High and Mystical Knowledge do immediately hearken unto the temptations of *Sathan*, and are misled by him into the Study of the *Black Art*. Hence it is that Magic lieth under disgrace, and they who seek after it are vulgarly esteemed *Sorcerers*.

The Fraternity of the Rosie Crusians thought it not fit to style themselves Magicians, but rather Philosophers. And they be not ignorant Empiricks,[12] but learned and experienced Physicians, whose remedies be not only Lawful but Divine.

𝕿𝖍𝖊 𝕭𝖗𝖎𝖊𝖋 𝕴𝖓𝖙𝖗𝖔𝖉𝖚𝖈𝖙𝖔𝖗𝖞 𝕯𝖊𝖘𝖈𝖗𝖎𝖕𝖙𝖎𝖔𝖓

(N.B. This is taken from several MS. Codices, of which the four principal variations are here composed together in parallel columns as an example of the close agreement of the various texts of the Lemegeton.

For in the whole work the differences in the wording of the various Codices are not sufficient to require the constant giving of parallel readings; but except in the more ancient examples there is much deterioration in the Seals and Sigils, so that in this latter respect the more recent exemplars are not entirely reliable.)

---

[11] Or the Black Art, as distinct from mere Necromancy, or Divination by the Dead.

[12] Or Quacks and Pretenders.

Clavicula Salomonis Regis,

which containeth all the Names, Offices, and Orders of all the Spirits that ever he had converse with, with the Seals and Characters to each Spirit and the manner of calling them forth to visible appearance:

In 5 parts, viz.:

(1) THE FIRST PART is a Book of Evil Spirits, called GOETIA, showing how he bound up those Spirits, and used them in general things, whereby he obtained great fame.

(2) THE SECOND PART is a Book of Spirits, partly Evil and partly Good, which is named THEURGIA-GOETIA, all Aërial Spirits, etc.

(3) THE THIRD PART is of Spirits governing the Planetary Hours, and what Spirits belong to every degree, of the Signs, and Planets in the Signs. Called the PAULINE ART, etc.

(4) THE FOURTH PART of this Book is called ALMADEL or SOLOMON, which containeth those Spirits which govern the Four Altitudes, or the 360 Degrees of the Zodiac.

These two last Orders of Spirits are Good, and to be sought for by Divine seeking, etc., and are called THEURGIA.

(5) THE FIFTH PART is a Book of Orations and Prayers that Wise Solomon used upon the Altar in the Temple. The which is called ARS NOVA, which was revealed unto Solomon by that Holy Angel of God called MICHAEL; and he also received many brief Notes written with the Finger of God, which were declared to him by the said Angel with Claps of Thunder; without which Notes King Solomon had never obtained his great knowledge, for by them in a short time he knew all Arts and Sciences both Good and Bad; from these Notes it is called the NOTARY ART, etc.

The Whole Lemegeton Or Clavicula.

Now this Book containeth all the Names, Orders, and Offices of all the Spirits with which Solomon ever conversed, the Seals and Characters belonging to each Spirit, and the manner of calling them forth to visible appearance:

Divided into 5 special Books or parts, viz.:

(1) THE FIRST BOOK, or PART, which is a Book concerning Spirits of Evil, and which is termed THE GOETIA OF SOLOMON, sheweth forth his manner of binding these Spirits for use in things divers. And hereby did he acquire great renown.

(2) THE SECOND BOOK is one which treateth of Spirits mingled of Good and Evil Natures, the which is entitled THE THEURGIA-GOETIA, or the Magical Wisdom of the Spirits Aërial, whereof some do abide, but certain do wander and abide not.

(3) THE THIRD BOOK, called ARS PAULINA, or THE ART PAULINE, treateth of the Spirits allotted unto every degree of the 360 Degrees of the Zodiac; and also of the Signs, and of the Planets in the Signs, as well as of the Hours.

(4) THE FOURTH BOOK, called ARS ALMADEL SALOMONIS, or THE ART ALMADEL OF SOLOMON, concerneth those Spirits which be set over the Quaternary of the Altitudes.

These two last mentioned Books, the ART PAULINE and the ART ALMADEL, do relate unto Good Spirits alone, whose knowledge is to be obtained through seeking unto the Divine. These two Books be also classed together under the Name of the First and Second Parts of the Book THEURGIA OF SOLOMON.

(5) THE FIFTH BOOK of the Lemegeton is one of Prayers and Orations. The which Solomon the Wise did use upon the Altar in the Temple. And the titles hereof be ARS NOVA, the NEW ART, and ARS NOTARIA, the NOTARY ART. The which was revealed to him by MICHAEL, that Holy Angel of God, in thunder and in

lightning, and he further did receive by the aforesaid Angel certain Notes written by the Hand of God, without the which that Great King had never attained unto his great Wisdom, for thus he knew all things and all Sciences and Arts whether Good or Evil.

Clabicula Salomonis Regis,

  which containeth all the Names, Offices, and Orders of all the Spirits with. whom he ever held any converse; together with the Seals and Characters proper unto each Spirit, and the method of calling them forth to visible appearance:

  In 5 parts, viz.:

(1) THE FIRST PART is a Book of Evil Spirits, called GOETIA, showing how he bound up those Spirits and used them in things general and several, whereby be obtained great fame.

(2) THE SECOND PART is a Book of Spirits, partly Evil and partly Good, which is called THEURGIA-GOETIA, all Aërial Spirits, etc.

(3) THE THIRD PART is of Spirits governing the Planetary Hours, and of what Spirits do belong to every Degree of the Signs, and of the Planets in the Signs. This is called the PAULINE ART, etc.

(4) THE FOURTH PART of this Book is called ALMADEL OF SOLOMON, the which containeth those Spirits which do govern the Four Altitudes, or the 360 Degrees of the Zodiac.

These two last Orders of Spirits are Good, and are called THEUR-GIA, and are to be sought for by Divine seeking, etc.

(5) THE FIFTH PART is a Book of Orations and Prayers which Wise Solomon did use upon the Altar in the Temple. The which is called ARS NOVA, the which was revealed to Solomon by that Holy Angel of God called Michael; and he also received many brief Notes written with the Finger of God, which were declared to him by the said Angel with Claps of Thunder; without which Notes King Solomon had never obtained his Great Wisdom, for by them in short

time he gained Knowledge of all Arts and Sciences both Good and Bad; from these Notes it is called the NOTARY ART, etc.

The Book Of Evil Spirits

THE KEY OF SOLOMON, which contains all the names, orders, and offices of all the Spirits that ever Solomon conversed with, together with the Seals and Characters belonging to each Spirit, and the manner of calling them forth to visible appearance:

In 4 parts.

(1) THE FIRST PART is a Book of Evil Spirits, called GOETIA, showing how he bound up those Spirits and used them in several things, whereby he obtained great fame.

(2) THE SECOND PART is a Book of Spirits, partly Good and partly Evil, which is named THEURGIA-GOETIA, all Aërial Spirits, etc.

(3) THE: THIRD PART is a Book governing the Planetary Houses, and what Spirits belong to every Degree of the Signs, and Planets in the Signs. Called the Pauline Art.

(4) THE FOURTH PART is a Book called the ALMADEL OF SOLOMON, which contains Twenty Chief Spirits who govern the Four Altitudes, or the 360 Degrees of the Zodiac.

These two last Orders of Spirits are Good, and called THEURGIA, and are to be sought after by Divine seeking.

These Most Sacred Mysteries were revealed unto Solomon.

Now in this Book LEMEGETON is contained the whole Art of King Solomon. And although there be many other Books that are said to be his, yet none is to be compared hereunto, for this containeth them all. Though there be titles with several other Names of the Book, as THE BOOK HELISOL, which is the very same with this last Book of Lemegeton called ARS NOVA or ARS NOTARIA, etc.

These Books were first found in the Chaldee and Hebrew Tongues at Jerusalem by a Jewish Rabbi; and by him put into the Greek language and thence into the Latin, as it is said.

Shemhamphorash

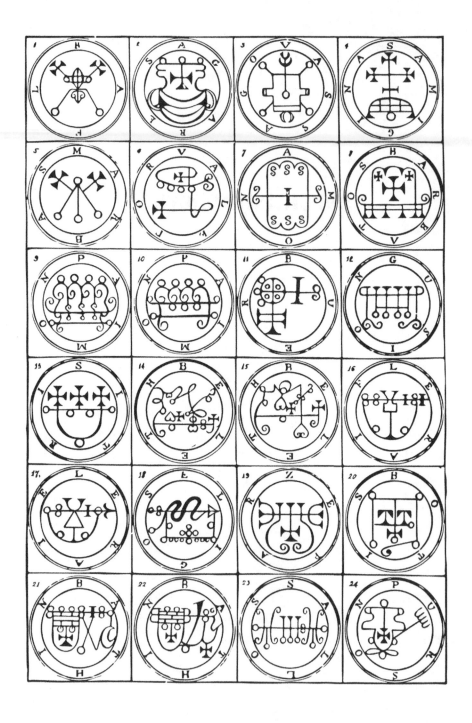

(1.) BAEL.--The First Principal Spirit is a King ruling in the East, called Bael. He maketh thee to go Invisible. He ruleth over 66 Legions of Infernal Spirits. He appeareth in divers shapes, sometimes like a Cat, sometimes like a Toad, and sometimes like a Man, and sometimes all these forms at once. He speaketh hoarsely. This is his character which is used to be worn as a Lamen before him who calleth him forth, or else he will not do thee homage.

(2.) AGARES.--The Second Spirit is a Duke called Agreas, or Agares. He is under the Power of the East, and cometh up in the form of an old fair Man, riding upon a Crocodile, carrying a Goshawk upon his fist, and yet mild in appearance. He maketh them to run that stand still, and bringeth back runaways. He teaches all Languages or Tongues presently. He hath power also to destroy Dignities both Spiritual and Temporal, and causeth Earthquakes. He was of the Order of Virtues. He hath under his government 31 Legions of Spirits. And this is his Seal or Character which thou shalt wear as a Lamen before thee.

(3.) VASSAGO.--The Third Spirit is a Mighty Prince, being of the same nature as Agares. He is called Vassago. This Spirit is of a Good Nature, and his office is to declare things Past and to Come, and to discover all things Hid or Lost. And he governeth 26 Legions of Spirits, and this is his Seal.

(4.) SAMIGINA, or GAMIGM.--The Fourth Spirit is Samigina, a Great Marquis. He appeareth in the form of a little Horse or Ass, and then into Human shape doth he change himself at the request of the Master. He speaketh with a hoarse voice. He ruleth over 30 Legions of Inferiors. He teaches all Liberal Sciences, and giveth account of Dead Souls that died in sin. And his Seal is this, which is to be worn before the Magician when he is Invocator, etc.

(5.) MARBAS.--The fifth Spirit is Marbas. He is a Great President, and appeareth at first in the form of a Great Lion, but afterwards, at the request of the Master, he putteth on Human Shape. He answereth truly of things Hidden or Secret. He causeth Diseases and cureth them. Again, he giveth great Wisdom and Knowledge in Mechanical Arts; and can change men into other shapes. He governeth 36 Legions of Spirits. And his Seal is this, which is to be worn as aforesaid.

(6.) VALEFOR.--The Sixth Spirit is Valefor. He is a mighty Duke, and appeareth in the shape of a Lion with an Ass's Head, bellowing. He is a good Familiar, but tempteth them he is a familiar of to steal. He governeth 10 Legions of Spirits. His Seal is this, which is to be worn, whether thou wilt have him for a Familiar, or not.

(7.) AMON.--The Seventh Spirit is Amon. He is a Marquis great in power, and most stern. He appeareth like a Wolf with a Serpents tail, vomiting out of his mouth flames of fire; but at the command of the Magician he putteth on the shape of a Man with Dog's teeth beset in a head like a Raven; or else like a Man with a Raven's head (simply). He telleth all things Past and to Come. He procureth feuds and reconcileth controversies between friends. He governeth 40 Legions of Spirits. His Seal is this which is to be worn as aforesaid, etc.

(8.) BARBATOS.--The Eighth Spirit is Barbatos. He is a Great Duke, and appeareth when the Sun is in Sagittary, with four noble Kings and their companies of great troops. He giveth understanding of the singing of Birds, and of the Voices of other creatures, such as the barking of Dogs. He breaketh the Hidden Treasures open that have been laid by the Enchantments of Magicians. He is of the Order of Virtues, of which some part he retaineth still; and he knoweth all things Past, and to come, and conciliateth Friends and those that be in Power. He ruleth over 30 Legions of Spirits. His Seal of Obedience is this, the which wear before thee as aforesaid.

(9) PAIMON.~The Ninth Spirit in this Order is Paimon, a Great King, and very obedient unto LUCIFER. He appeareth in the form of a Man sitting upon a Dromedary with a Crown most glorious upon his head. There goeth before him also an Host of Spirits, like Men with Trumpets and well sounding Cymbals, and all other sorts of Musical Instruments. He hath a great Voice, and roareth at his first coming, and his speech is such that the Magician cannot well understand unless he can compel him. This Spirit can teach all Arts and Sciences, and other secret things. He can discover unto thee what the Earth is, and what holdeth it up in the Waters; and what Mind is, and where it is; or any other thing thou mayest desire to know. He giveth Dignity, and confirmeth the same. He bindeth or maketh any man subject unto the Magician if he so desire it. He giveth good Familiars, and such as can teach all Arts. He is to be observed towards the West. He is of the Order of Dominations.[13] He hath under him 200 Legions of Spirits, and part of them are of the Order of Angels, and the other part of Potentates. Now if thou callest this Spirit Paimon alone, thou must make him some offering; and there will attend him two Kings called LABAL and ABALIM, and also other Spirits who be of the Order of Potentates in his Host, and 25 Legions. And those Spirits which be subject unto them are not always with them unless the Magician do compel them. His Character is this which must be worn as a Lamen before thee, etc.

(10.) BUER.~The Tenth Spirit is Buer, a Great President. He appeareth in Sagittary, and that is his shape when the Sun is there. He teaches Philosophy, both Moral and Natural, and the Logic Art, and also the Virtues of all Herbs and Plants. He healeth all distempers in man, and giveth good Familiars. He governeth 50 Legions of Spirits, and his Character of obedience is this, which thou must wear when thou callest him forth unto appearance.

---

[13] Or Dominions, as they are usually termed.

(11.) GUSION.~The Eleventh Spirit in order is a great and strong Duke, called Gusion. He appeareth like a Xenopilus. He telleth all things, Past, Present, and to Come, and showeth the meaning and resolution of all questions thou mayest ask. He conciliateth and reconcileth friendships, and giveth Honour and Dignity unto any. He ruleth over 40 Legions of Spirits. His Seal is this, the which wear thou as aforesaid.

(12.) SITRI.~The Twelfth Spirit is Sitri. He is a Great Prince and appeareth at first with a Leopard's head and the Wings of a Gryphon, but after the command of the Master of the Exorcism he putteth on Human shape, and that very beautiful. He enflameth men with Women's love, and Women with Men's love; and causeth them also to show themselves naked if it be desired. He governeth 60 Legions of Spirits. His Seal is this, to be worn as a Lamen before thee, etc.

(13.) BELETH.~The Thirteenth Spirit is called Beleth (or Bileth, or Bilet). He is a mighty King and terrible. He rideth on a pale horse with trumpets and other kinds of musical instruments playing before him. He is very furious at his first appearance, that is, while the Exorcist layeth his courage; for to do this he must hold a Hazel Wand in his hand, striking it out towards the South and East Quarters, make a triangle, $\triangle$, without the Circle, and then command him into it by the Bonds and Charges of Spirits as hereafter followeth. And if he doth not enter into the triangle, $\triangle$, at your threats, rehearse the Bonds and Charms before him, and then he will yield Obedience and come into it, and do what he is commanded by the Exorcist. Yet he must receive him courteously because he is a Great King, and do homage unto him, as the Kings and Princes do that attend upon him. And thou must have always a Silver Ring on the middle finger of the left hand held against thy face,[14] as they do yet before AMAYMON. This Great King Beleth causeth all the love that may be, both of Men and of Women, until the Master Exorcist hath had his desire fulfilled. He is of the Order of Powers, and he governeth 85 Legions of Spirits. His Noble Seal is this, which is to be worn before thee at working.

(14.) LERAJE, or LERAIKHA.~The Fourteenth Spirit is called Leraje (or Leraie). He is a Marquis Great in Power, showing himself in the likeness of an Archer clad in Green, and carrying a Bow and Quiver. He causeth all great Battles and Contests; and maketh wounds to putrefy that are made with Arrows by Archers. This belongeth unto Sagittary. He governeth 30 Legions of Spirits, and this is his Seal, etc.

(15.) ELIGOS.~The Fifteenth Spirit in Order is Eligos, a Great Duke, and appeareth in the form of a goodly Knight, carrying a Lance, an Ensign, and a Serpent. He discovereth hidden things, and knoweth things to come; and of Wars, and how the Soldiers will or shall meet. He causeth the Love of Lords and Great Persons. He governeth 60 Legions of Spirits. His Seal is this, etc.

(16.) ZEPAR.~The Sixteenth Spirit is Zepar. He is a Great Duke, and appeareth in Red Apparel and Armour, like a Soldier. His office is to cause Women to love Men, and to bring them together in love. He also maketh them barren. He governeth 26 Legions of Inferior Spirits, and his Seal is this, which he obeyeth when he seeth it.

(17.) BOTIS.~The Seventeenth Spirit is Botis, a Great President, and an Earl. He appeareth at the first show in the form of an ugly Viper, then at the command of the Magician he putteth on a Human shape with Great Teeth, and two Horns, carrying a bright and sharp Sword in his hand. He telleth all things Past, and to Come,

---

[14] To protect him from the flaming breath of the enraged Spirit; the design is given at the end of the instructions for the Magical Circle, etc., later on in the Goetia.

and reconcileth Friends and Foes. He ruleth over 60 Legions of Spirits, and this is his Seal, etc.

(18.) BATHIN.~The Eighteenth Spirit is Bathin. He is a Mighty and Strong Duke, and appeareth like a Strong Man with the tail of a Serpent, sitting upon a Pale-Coloured Horse. He knoweth the Virtues of Herbs and Precious Stones, and can transport men suddenly from one country to another. He ruleth over 30 Legions of Spirits. His Seal is this which is to be worn as aforesaid.

(19.) SALLOS.~The Nineteenth Spirit is Sallos (or Saleos). He is a Great and Mighty Duke, and appeareth in the form of a gallant Soldier riding on a Crocodile, with a Ducal Crown on his head, but peaceably. He causeth the Love of Women to Men, and of Men to Women; and governeth 30 Legions of Spirits. His Seal is this, etc.

(20.) PURSON.~The Twentieth Spirit is Purson, a Great King. His appearance is comely, like a Man with a Lion's face, carrying a cruel Viper in his hand, and riding upon a Bear. Going before him are many Trumpets sounding. He knoweth all things hidden, and can discover Treasure, and tell all things Past, Present, and to Come. He can take a Body either Human or Aërial, and answereth truly of all Earthly things both Secret and Divine, and of the Creation of the World. He bringeth forth good Familiars, and under his Government there be 22 Legions of Spirits, partly of the Order of Virtues and partly of the Order of Thrones. His Mark, Seal, or Character is this, unto the which he oweth obedience, and which thou shalt wear in time of action, etc.

(21.) MARAX.~The Twenty-first Spirit is Marax.[15] He is a Great Earl and President. He appeareth like a great Bull with a Man's face. His office is to make Men very knowing in Astronomy, and all other Liberal Sciences; also he can give good Familiars, and wise, knowing the virtues of Herbs and Stones which be precious. He governeth

---

[15] In some Codices written Morax, but I consider the above the correct orthography.

30 Legions of Spirits, and his Seal is this, which must be made and worn as aforesaid, etc.

(22.) IPOS.--The Twenty-second Spirit is Ipos. He is an Earl, and a Mighty Prince, and appeareth in the form of an Angel with a Lion's Head, and a Goose's Foot, and Hare's Tail. He knoweth all things Past, Present, and to Come. He maketh men witty and bold.

He governeth 36 Legions of Spirits. His Seal is this, which thou shalt wear, etc.

(23.) AIM.--The Twenty-third Spirit is Aim. He is a Great Strong Duke. He appeareth in the form of a very handsome Man in body, but with three Heads; the first, like a Serpent, the second like a Man having two Stars on his Forehead, the third like a Calf. He rideth on a Viper, carrying a Firebrand in his Hand, wherewith he setteth cities, castles, and great Places, on fire. He maketh thee witty in all manner of ways, and giveth true answers unto private matters. He governeth 26 Legions of Inferior Spirits; and his Seal is this, which wear thou as aforesaid, etc.

(24.) NABERIUS.--The Twenty-fourth Spirit is Naberius. He is a most valiant Marquis, and showeth in the form of a Black Crane, fluttering about the Circle, and when he speaketh it is with a hoarse voice. He maketh men cunning in all Arts and Sciences, but especially in the Art of Rhetoric. He restoreth lost Dignities and Honours. He governeth 19 Legions of Spirits. His Seal is this, which is to be worn, etc.

(25.) GLASYA-LABOLAS.--The Twenty-fifth Spirit is Glasya-Labolas. He is a Mighty President and Earl, and showeth himself in the form of a Dog with Wings like a Gryphon. He teacheth all Arts and Sciences in an instant, and is an Author of Bloodshed and Manslaughter. He teacheth all things Past, and to Come. If desired he causeth the love both of Friends and of Foes. He can make a Man to go Invisible. And he hath under his command 36 Legions of Spirits. His Seal is this, to be, etc.

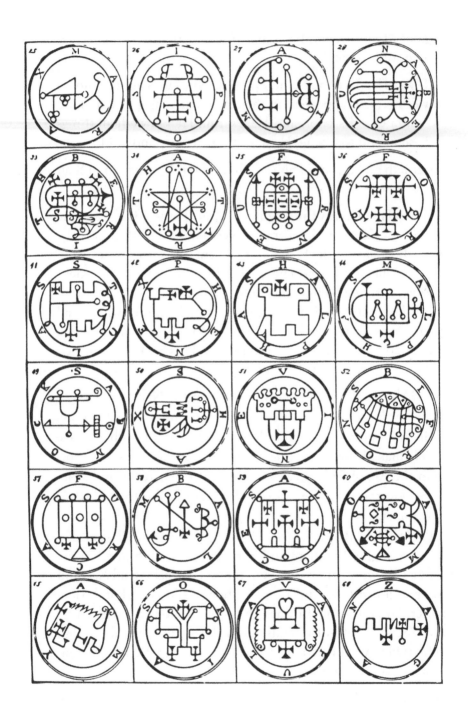

(26.) BUNE, or BIMÉ.~The Twenty-sixth Spirit is Buné (or Bim). He is a Strong, Great and Mighty Duke. He appeareth in the form of a Dragon with three heads, one like a Dog, one like a Gryphon, and one like a Man. He speaketh with a high and comely Voice. He changeth the Place of the Dead, and causeth the Spirits which be under him to gather together upon your Sepulchres. He giveth Riches unto a Man, and maketh him Wise and Eloquent. He giveth true Answers unto Demands. And he governeth 30 Legions of Spirits. His Seal is this, unto the which he oweth Obedience. He hath another Seal (which is the first of these,[16] but the last is the best)[17].

(27.) RONOVÉ.~The Twenty-seventh Spirit is Ronové. He appeareth in the Form of a Monster. He teacheth the Art of Rhetoric very well and giveth Good Servants, Knowledge of Tongues, and Favours with Friends or Foes. He is a Marquis and Great Earl; and there be under his command 19 Legions of Spirits. His Seal is this, etc.

(28.) BERITH.~The Twenty-eighth Spirit in Order, as Solomon bound them, is named Berith. He is a Mighty, Great, and Terrible Duke. He hath two other Names given unto him by men of later times, viz.: BEALE, or BEAL, and BOFRY or BOLFRY. He appeareth in the Form of a Soldier with Red Clothing, riding upon a Red Horse, and having a Crown of Gold upon his head. He giveth true answers, Past, Present, and to Come. Thou must make use of a Ring in calling him forth, as is before spoken of regarding Beleth.[18] He can turn all metals into Gold. He can give Dignities, and can confirm them unto Man. He speaketh with a very clear and subtle Voice. He governeth 26 Legions of Spirits. His Seal is this, etc.

---

[16] Figure 30.
[17] Figure 31.
[18] See *ante*, Spirit No. 13.

(29.) ASTAROTH.-The Twenty.-ninth Spirit is Astaroth. He is a Mighty, Strong Duke, and appeareth in the Form of an hurtful Angel riding on an Infernal Beast like a Dragon, and carrying in his right hand a Viper. Thou must in no wise let him approach too near unto thee, lest he do thee damage by his Noisome Breath. Wherefore the Magician must hold the Magical Ring near his face, and that will defend him. He giveth true answers of things Past, Present, and to Come, and can discover all Secrets. He will declare wittingly how the Spirits fell, if desired, and the reason of his own fall. He can make men wonderfully knowing in all Liberal Sciences. He ruleth 40 Legions of Spirits. His Seal is this, which wear thou as a Lamen before thee, or else he will not appear nor yet obey thee, etc.

(30.) FORNEUS.-The Thirtieth Spirit is Forneus. He is a Mighty and Great Marquis, and appeareth in the Form of a Great Sea-Monster. He teacheth, and maketh men wonderfully knowing in the Art of Rhetoric. He causeth men to have a Good Name, and to have the knowledge and understanding of Tongues. He maketh one to be beloved of his Foes as well as of his Friends. He governeth 29 Legions of Spirits, partly of the Order of Thrones, and partly of that of Angels. His Seal is this, which wear thou, etc.

(31.) FORAS.-The Thirty-first Spirit is Foras. He is a Mighty President, and appeareth in the Form of a Strong Man in Human Shape. He can give the understanding to Men how they may know the Virtues of all Herbs and Precious Stones. He teacheth the Arts of Logic and Ethics in all their parts. If desired he maketh men invisible,[19] and to live long, and to be eloquent. He can discover Treasures and recover things Lost. He ruleth over 29 Legions of Spirits, and his Seal is this, which wear thou, etc.

------

[19] One or two Codices have "invincible," but "invisible" is given in the majority. Yet the form of appearance of Foras as a strong man might warrant the former, though from the nature of his offices the invincibility would probably be rather on the mental than on the physical plane.

(32.) ASMODAY.--The Thirty-second Spirit is Asmoday, or Asmodai. He is a Great King, Strong, and Powerful. He appeareth with Three Heads, whereof the first is like a Bull, the second like a Man, and the third like a Ram; he bath also the tail of a Serpent, and from his mouth issue Flames of Fire. His Feet are webbed like those of a Goose. He sitteth upon an Infernal Dragon, and beareth in his hand a Lance with a Banner. He is first and choicest under the Power of AMAYMON, he goeth before all other. When the Exorcist bath a mind to call him, let it be abroad, and let him stand on his feet all the time of action, with his Cap or Headdress off; for if it be on, AMAYMON will deceive him and call all his actions to be bewrayed. But as soon as the Exorcist seeth Asmoday in the shape aforesaid, he shall call him by his Name, saying: "Art thou Asmoday?" and he will not deny it, and by-and-by he will bow down unto the ground. He giveth the Ring of Virtues; he teacheth the Arts of Arithmetic, Astronomy, Geometry, and all handicrafts absolutely. He giveth true and full answers unto thy demands. He maketh one Invincible. He showeth the place where Treasures lie, and guardeth it. He, amongst the Legions of AMAYMON governeth 72 Legions of Spirits Inferior. His Seal is this which thou must wear as a Lamen upon thy breast, etc.

(33.) GAAP.--The Thirty-third Spirit is Gaap. He is a Great President and a Mighty Prince. He appeareth when the Sun is in some of the Southern Signs, in a Human Shape, going before Four Great and Mighty Kings, as if he were a Guide to conduct them along on their way. His Office is to make men Insensible or Ignorant; as also in Philosophy to make them Knowing, and in all the Liberal Sciences. He can cause Love or Hatred, also he can teach thee to consecrate those things that belong to the Dominion of AMAYMON his King. He can deliver Familiars out of the Custody of other Magicians, and answereth truly and perfectly of things Past, Present, and to Come. He can carry and re-carry men very speedily from one Kingdom to another, at the Will and Pleasure of the Exorcist. He ruleth over 66 Legions of Spirits, and he was of the Order of Potentates. His Seal is this to be made and to be worn as aforesaid, etc.

(34.) FURFUR.-The Thirty-fourth Spirit is Furfur. He is a Great and Mighty Earl, appearing in the Form of an Hart with a Fiery Tail. He never speaketh truth unless he be compelled, or brought up within a triangle, $\triangle$. Being therein, he will take upon himself the Form of an Angel. Being bidden, he speaketh with a hoarse voice. Also he will wittingly urge Love between Man and Woman. He can raise Lightnings and Thunders, Blasts, and Great Tempestuous Storms. And he giveth True Answers both of Things Secret and Divine, if commanded. He ruleth over 26 Legions of Spirits. And his Seal is this, etc.

(35.) MARCHOSIAS.-The Thirty-fifth Spirit is Marchosias. He is a Great and Mighty Marquis, appearing at first in the Form of a Wolf[20] having Gryphon's Wings, and a Serpent's Tail, and Vomiting Fire out of his mouth. But after a time, at the command of the Exorcist he putteth on the Shape of a Man. And be is a strong fighter. He was of the Order of Dominations. He governeth 30 Legions of Spirits. He told his Chief, who was Solomon, that after 1,200 years he had hopes to return unto the Seventh Throne. And his Seal is this, to be made and worn as a Lamen, etc.

(36.) STOLAS, OR STOLOS.-The Thirty-sixth Spirit is Stolas, or Stolos. He is a Great and Powerful Prince, appearing in the Shape of a Mighty Raven at first before the Exorcist; but after he taketh the image of a Man. He teacheth the Art of Astronomy, and the Virtues of Herbs and Precious Stones. He governeth 26 Legions of Spirits; and his Seal is this, which is, etc.

(37.) PHENEX.-The Thirty-Seventh Spirit is Phenex (or Pheynix). He is a great Marquis, and appeareth like the Bird Phoenix, having

---

[20] On one Codex of the seventeenth century, very badly written, it might be read "Ox" instead of "Wolf."-TRANS. [For me he appeared always like an ox, and very dazed.-ED.]

the Voice of a Child. He singeth many sweet notes before the Exorcist, which he must not regard, but by-and-by he must bid him put on Human Shape. Then he will speak marvellously of all wonderful Sciences if required. He is a Poet, good and excellent. And he will be willing to perform thy requests. He hath hopes also to return to the Seventh Throne after 1,200 years more, as he said unto Solomon. He governeth 20 Legions of Spirits. And his Seal is this, which wear thou, etc.

(38.) HALPHAS, or MALTHUS.--The Thirty-eighth Spirit is Halphas, or Malthous (or Malthas). He is a Great Earl, and appeareth in the Form of a Stock-Dove. He speaketh with a hoarse Voice. His Office is to build up Towers, and to furnish them with Ammunition and Weapons, and to send Men-of-War[21] to places appointed. He ruleth over 26 Legions of Spirits, and his Seal is this, etc.

(39.) MALPHAS.--The Thirty-ninth Spirit is Malphas. He appeareth at first like a Crow, but after he will put on Human Shape at the request of the Exorcist, and speak with a hoarse Voice. He is a Mighty President and Powerful. He can build Houses and High Towers, and can bring to thy Knowledge Enemies' Desires and Thoughts, and that which they have done. He giveth Good Familiars. If thou makest a Sacrifice unto him he will receive it kindly and willingly, but he will deceive him that doth it. He governeth 40 Legions of Spirits, and his Seal is this, etc.

(40.) RAUM.--The Fortieth Spirit is Räum. He is a Great Earl; and appeareth at first in the Form of a Crow, but after the Command of the Exorcist he putteth on Human Shape. His office is to steal Treasures out King's Houses, and to carry it whither he is commanded, and to destroy Cities and Dignities of Men, and to tell all things, Past, and What Is, and what Will Be; and to cause Love between Friends and Foes. He was of the Order of Thrones. He

---

[21] Or Warriors, or Men-at-Arms.

governeth 30 Legions of Spirits; and his Seal is this, which wear thou as aforesaid.

(41.) FOCALOR.--The Forty-first Spirit is Focalor, or Forcalor, or Furcalor. He is a Mighty Duke and Strong. He appeareth in the Form of a Man with Gryphon's Wings. His office is to slay Men, and to drown them in the Waters, and to overthrow Ships of War, for he hath Power over both Winds and Seas; but he will not hurt any man or thing if he be commanded to the contrary by the Exorcist. He also hath hopes to return to the Seventh Throne after 1,000 years. He governeth 30 Legions of Spirits, and his Seal is this, etc.

(42.) VEPAR.--The Forty-second Spirit is Vepar, or Vephar. He is a Duke Great and Strong and appeareth like a Mermaid. His office is to govern the Waters, and to guide Ships laden with Arms, Armour, and Ammunition, etc., thereon. And at the request of the Exorcist he can cause the seas to be right stormy and to appear

full of ships. Also he maketh men to die in Three Days by Putrefying Wounds or Sores, and causing Worms to breed in them. He governeth 29 Legions of Spirits, and his Seal is this, etc.

(43.) SABNOCK.--The Forty-third Spirit, as King Solomon commanded them into the Vessel of Brass, is called Sabnock, or Savnok. He is a Marquis, Mighty, Great and Strong, appearing in the Form of an Armed Soldier with a Lion's Head, riding on a pale-coloured horse. His office is to build high Towers, Castles and Cities, and to furnish them with Armour, etc. Also he can afflict Men for many days with Wounds and with Sores rotten and full of Worms. He giveth Good Familiars at the request of the Exorcist. He commandeth 50 Legions of Spirits; and his Seal is this, etc.

(44.) SHAN.--The Forty-fourth Spirit is Shax, or Shaz (or Shass). He is a Great Marquis and appeareth in the Form of a Stock-Dove, speaking with a voice hoarse, but yet subtle. His Office is to take away the Sight, Hearing, or Understanding of any Man or Woman at the command of the Exorcist; and to steal money out of the houses of Kings, and to carry it again in 1,200 years. If commanded he will fetch Horses at the request of the Exorcist, or any other thing. But he must first be commanded into a Triangle, Δ, or else he will deceive him, and tell him many Lies. He can discover all things that are Hidden, and not kept by Wicked Spirits. He giveth good Familiars, sometimes. He governeth 30 Legions of Spirits, and his Seal is this, etc.

(45.) VINÉ.--The Forty-fifth Spirit is Viné, or Vinea. He is a Great King, and an Earl; and appeareth in the Form of a Lion,[22] riding upon a Black Horse, and bearing a Viper in his hand. His Office is to discover Things Hidden, Witches, Wizards, and Things Present, Past, and to Come. He, at the command of the Exorcist will build Towers, overthrow Great Stone Walls, and make the Waters rough with Storms. He governeth 36 Legions of Spirits. And his Seal is this, which wear thou, as aforesaid, etc.

(46.) BIFRONS.--The Forty-sixth Spirit is called Bifrons, or Bifröus, or Bifrovs. He is an Earl, and appeareth in the Form of a Monster; but after a while, at the Command of the Exorcist, he putteth on the shape of a Man. His Office is to make one knowing in Astrology, Geometry, and other Arts and Sciences. He teacheth the Virtues of Precious Stones and Woods. He changeth Dead Bodies, and putteth them in another place; also he lighteth seeming Candles upon the Graves of the Dead. He hath under his Command 6 Legions of Spirits. His Seal is this, which he will own and submit unto, etc.

(47.) UVALL, VUAL, or VOVAL.--The Forty-seventh Spirit Uvall, or Vual, or Voval. He is a Duke, Great, Mighty, and Strong; and appeareth in the Form of a Mighty Dromedary at the first, but after a while at the Command of the Exorcist he putteth on Human Shape, and speaketh the Egyptian Tongue, but not perfectly.[23] His

---

[22] Or with the Head of a Lion, or having a Lion's Head, in some Codices.

[23] He can nowadays converse in sound though colloquial Coptic.--ED.

Office is to procure the Love of Woman, and to tell Things Past, Present, and to Come. He also procureth Friendship between Friends and Foes. He was of the Order of Potestates or Powers. He governeth 37 Legions of Spirits, and his Seal is this, to be made and worn before thee, etc.

(48.) HAAGENTI.~The Forty-eighth Spirit is Haagenti. He is a President, appearing in the Form of a Mighty Bull with Gryphon's Wings. This is at first, but after, at the Command of the Exorcist he putteth on Human Shape. His Office is to make Men wise, and to instruct them in divers things; also to Transmute all Metals into Gold; and to change Wine into Water, and Water into Wine. He governeth 33 Legions of Spirits, and his Seal is this, etc.

(49.) CROCELL.~The Forty-ninth Spirit is Crocell, or Crokel. He appeareth in the Form of an Angel. He is a Duke Great and Strong, speaking something Mystically of Hidden Things. He teacheth the Art of Geometry and the Liberal Sciences. He, at the Command of the Exorcist, will produce Great Noises like the Rushings of many Waters, although there be none. He warmeth Waters, and discovereth Baths. He was of the Order of Potestates, or Powers, before his fall, as he declared unto the King Solomon. He governeth 48 Legions of Spirits. His Seal is this, the which wear thou as aforesaid.

(50.) FURCAS.~The Fiftieth Spirit is Furcas. He is a Knight, and appeareth in the Form of a Cruel Old Man with a long Beard and a hoary Head, riding upon a pale-coloured Horse, with a Sharp Weapon in his hand. His Office is to teach the Arts of Philosophy, Astrology, Rhetoric, Logic, Cheiromancy, and Pyromancy, in all their parts, and perfectly. He hath under his Power 20 Legions of Spirits. His Seal, or Mark, is thus made, etc.

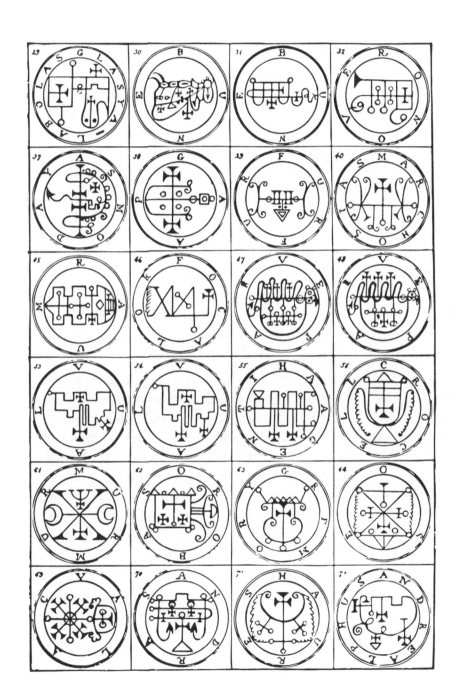

(51.) BALAM.~The Fifty-first Spirit is Balam or Balaam. He is a Terrible, Great, and Powerful King. He appeareth with three Heads: the first is like that of a Bull; the second is like that of a Man; the third is like that of a Ram. He hath the Tail of a Serpent, and Flaming Eyes. He rideth upon a furious Bear, and carrieth a Boshawk upon his Fist. He speaketh with a hoarse Voice, giving True Answers of Things Past, Present, and to Come. He maketh men to go Invisible, and also to be Witty. He governeth 40 Legions of Spirits. His Seal is this, etc.

(52.) ALLOCES.~The Fifty-second Spirit is Alloces, or Alocas. He is a Duke, Great, Mighty, and Strong, appearing in the Form of a Soldier[24] riding upon a Great Horse. His Face is like that of a Lion, very Red, and having Flaming Eyes. His Speech is hoarse and very big.[25] His Office is to teach the Art of Astronomy, and all the Liberal Sciences. He bringeth unto thee Good Familiars; also he ruleth over 36 Legions of Spirits. His Seal is this, which, etc.

(53.) CAMIO or CAIM.~The Fifty-third Spirit is Camio, or Caim. He is a Great President, and appeareth in the Form of the Bird called a Thrush at first, but afterwards he putteth on the Shape of a Man carrying in his Hand a Sharp Sword. He seemeth to answer in Burning Ashes, or in Coals of Fire. He is a Good Disputer. His Office is to give unto Men the Understanding of all Birds, Lowing of Bullocks, Barking of Dogs, and other Creatures; and also of the Voice of the Waters. He giveth True Answers of Things to Come. He was of the Order of Angels, but now ruleth over 30 Legions of Spirits Infernal. His Seal is this, which wear thou, etc.

(54.) MURMUR, or MURMUS.~The Fifty-fourth Spirit is called Murmur, or Murmus, or Murmux. He is a Great Duke, and an Earl;

---

[24] Or Warrior.
[25] Thus expressed in the Codices.

and appeareth in the Form of a Warrior riding upon a Gryphon, with a Ducal Crown upon his Head. There do go before him those his Ministers with great Trumpets sounding. His Office is to teach Philosophy perfectly, and to constrain Souls Deceased to come before the Exorcist to answer those questions which he may wish to put to them, if desired. He was partly of the Order of Thrones, and partly of that of Angels. He now ruleth 30 Legions of Spirits. And his Seal is this, etc.

(55.) OROBAS.~The Fifty-fifth Spirit is Orobas. He is a great and Mighty Prince, appearing at first like a Horse; but after the command of the Exorcist he putteth on the Image of a Man. His Office is to discover all things Past, Present, and to Come; also to give Dignities, and Prelacies, and the Favour of Friends and of Foes. He giveth True Answers of Divinity, and of the Creation of the World. He is very faithful unto the Exorcist, and will not suffer him to be tempted of any Spirit. He governeth 20 Legions of Spirits. His Seal is this, etc.

(56) GREMORY, or GAMORI.~The Fifty-sixth Spirit is Gremory, or Gamori. He is a Duke Strong and Powerful, and appeareth in the Form of a Beautiful Woman, with a Duchess's Crown tied about her waist, and riding on a Great Camel. His Office is to tell of all Things Past, Present, and to Come; and of Treasures Rid, and what they lie in; and to procure the Love of Women both Young and Old. He governeth 26 Legions of Spirits, and his Seal is this, etc.

(57.) OSÉ, or VOSO.~The Fifty-seventh Spirit is Oso, Osé, or Voso. He is a Great President, and appeareth like a Leopard at the first, but after a little time he putteth on the Shape of a Man. His Office is to make one cunning in the Liberal Sciences, and to give True Answers of Divine and Secret Things; also to change a Man into any Shape that the Exorcist pleaseth, so that he that is so changed will not think any other thing than that he is in verity that Creature or

Thing he is changed into. He governeth 30[26] Legions of Spirits, and this is his Seal, etc.

(58.) AMY, or AVNAS.--The Fifty-eighth Spirit is Amy, or Avnas. He is a Great President, and appeareth at first in the Form of a Flaming Fire; but after a while he putteth on the Shape of a Man. His office is to make one Wonderful Knowing[27] in Astrology and all the Liberal Sciences. He giveth Good Familiars, and can bewray Treasure that is kept by Spirits. He governeth 36 Legions of Spirits, and his Seal is this, etc.

(59.) ORIAX, or ORIAS.--The Fifty-ninth Spirit is Oriax, or Orias. He is a Great Marquis, and appeareth in the Form of a Lion,[28] riding upon a Horse Mighty and Strong, with a Serpent's Tail;[29] and he holdeth in his Right Hand two Great Serpents hissing. His Office is to teach the Virtues of the Stars, and to know the Mansions of the Planets, and how to understand their Virtues. He also transformeth Men, and he giveth Dignities, Prelacies, and Confirmation thereof; also Favour with Friends and with Foes. He doth govern 30 Legions of Spirits; and his Seal is this, etc.

(60.) VAPULA, or NAPHULA.--The Sixtieth Spirit is Vapula, or Naphula. He is a Duke Great, Mighty, and Strong; appearing in the Form of a Lion with Gryphon's Wings. His Office is to make Men Knowing in all Handcrafts and Professions, also in Philosophy, and other Sciences. He governeth 36 Legions of Spirits, and his Seal or Character is thus made, and thou shalt wear it as aforesaid, etc.

(61.) ZAGAN.--The Sixty-first Spirit is Zagan. He is a Great King and President, appearing at first in the Form of a Bull with Gryphon's Wings; but after a while he putteth on Human Shape. He maketh

---

[26] Should be 30. For these 72 Great Spirits of the Book Goetia are all Princes and Leaders of numbers.

[27] Thus in the actual Text.

[28] Or "with the Face of a Lion."

[29] The horse, or the Markist?--ED.

Men Witty. He can turn Wine into Water, and Blood into Wine, also Water into Wine. He can turn all Metals into Coin of the Dominion that Metal is of. He can even make Fools wise. He governeth 33 Legions of Spirits, and his Seal is this, etc.

(62.) VOLAC, or VALAX, or VALU, or UALAC.~The Sixty-second Spirit is Volac, or Valak, or Valu. He is a President Mighty and Great, and appeareth like a Child with Angel's Wings, riding on a Two-headed Dragon. His Office is to give True Answers of Hidden Treasures, and to tell where Serpents may be seen. The which he will bring unto the Exorciser without any Force or Strength being by him employed. He governeth 38 Legions of Spirits, and his Seal is thus.

(63.) ANDRAS.~The Sixty-third Spirit is Andras. He is a Great Marquis, appearing in the Form of an Angel with a Head like a Black Night Raven, riding upon a strong Black Wolf, and having a Sharp and Bright Sword flourished aloft in his hand. His Office is to sow Discords. If the Exorcist have not a care, he will slay both him and his fellows. He governeth 30 Legions of Spirits, and this is his Seal, etc.

(64.) HAURES, or HAURAS, or HAVRES, or FLAUROS.~The Sixty-fourth Spirit is Haures, or Hauras, or Havres, or Flauros. He is a Great Duke, and appeareth at first like a Leopard, Mighty, Terrible, and Strong, but after a while, at the Command of the Exorcist, he putteth on Human Shape with Eyes Flaming and Fiery, and a most Terrible Countenance. He giveth True Answers of all things, Present, Past, and to Come. But if he be not commanded into a Triangle, Δ, he will Lie in all these Things, and deceive and beguile the Exorcist in these things, or in such and such business. He will, lastly, talk of the Creation of the World, and of Divinity, and of how he and other Spirits fell. He destroyeth and burneth up those who be the Enemies of the Exorcist should he so desire it; also he will not suffer him to be tempted by any other Spirit or otherwise.

He governeth 36 Legions of Spirits, and his Seal is this, to be worn as a Lamen, etc.

(65.) ANDREALPHUS.--The Sixty-fifth Spirit is Andrealphus. He is a Mighty Marquis, appearing at first in the form of a Peacock, with great Noises. But after a time he putteth on Human shape. He can teach Geometry perfectly. He maketh Men very subtle therein; and in all Things pertaining unto Mensuration or Astronomy. He can transform a Man into the Likeness of a Bird. He governeth 30 Legions of Infernal Spirits, and his Seal is this, etc.

(66.) CIMEJES, or CIMEIES, or KIMARIS.--The Sixty-sixth Spirit is Cimejes, or Cimeies, or Kimaris. He is a Marquis, Mighty, Great, Strong and Powerful, appearing like a Valiant Warrior riding upon a goodly Black Horse. He ruleth over all Spirits in the parts of Africa. His Office is to teach perfectly Grammar, Logic, Rhetoric, and to discover things Lost or Hidden, and Treasures. He governeth 20 Legions of Infernals; and his Seal is this, etc.

(67.) AMDUSIAS, or AMDUKIAS.--The Sixty-seventh Spirit is Amdusias, or Amdukias. He is a Duke Great and Strong, appearing at first like a Unicorn, but at the request of the Exorcist he standeth before him in Human Shape, causing Trumpets, and all manner of Musical Instruments to be heard, but not soon or immediately. Also he can cause Trees to bend and incline according to the Exorcist's Will. He giveth Excellent Familiars. He governeth 29 Legions of Spirits. And his Seal is this, etc.

(68.) BELIAL.--The Sixty-eighth Spirit is Belial. He is a Mighty and a Powerful King, and was created next after LUCIFER. He appeareth in the Form of Two Beautiful Angels sitting in a Chariot of Fire. He speaketh with a Comely Voice, and declareth that he fell first from among the worthier sort, that were before Michael, and other Heavenly Angels. His Office is to distribute Presentations and Senatorships, etc.; and to cause favour of Friends and of Foes. He giveth excellent Familiars, and governeth 50 Legions of Spirits. Note well that this King Belial. must have Offerings, Sacrifices and Gifts presented unto him by the Exorcist, or else he will not give True Answers unto his Demands. But then he tarrieth not one hour in the Truth, unless he be con. strained by Divine Power. And his Seal is this, which is to be worn as aforesaid, etc.

(69.) DECARABIA.-The Sixty-ninth Spirit is Decarabia. He appeareth in the Form of a Star in a Pentacle, at first; but after, at the command of the Exorcist, he putteth on the image of a Man. His Office is to discover the Virtues of Birds and Precious Stones, and to make the Similitude of all kinds of Birds to fly before the Exorcist, singing and drinking as natural Birds do. He governeth 30 Legions of Spirits, being himself a Great Marquis. And this is his Seal, which is to be worn, etc.

(70.) SEERE, SEAR, or SEIR.-The Seventieth Spirit is Seere, Sear, or Seir. He is a Mighty Prince, and Powerful, under AMAYMON, King of the East. He appeareth in the Form of a Beautiful Man, riding upon a Winged Horse. His Office is to go and come; and to bring abundance of things to pass on a sudden, and to carry or re-carry anything whither thou wouldest have it to go, or whence thou wouldest have it from. He can pass over the whole Earth in the twinkling of an Eye. He giveth a True relation of all sorts of Theft, and of Treasure hid, and of many other things. He is of an indifferent Good Nature, and is willing to do anything which the Exorcist desireth. He governeth 26 Legions of Spirits. And this his Seal is to be worn, etc.

(71.) DANTALION.-The Seventy-first Spirit is Dantalion. He is a Duke Great and Mighty, appearing in the Form of a Man with many Countenances, all Men's and Women's Faces; and he hath a Book in his right hand. His Office is to teach all Arts and Sciences unto any; and to declare the Secret Counsel of any one; for he knoweth the Thoughts of all Men and Women, and can change them at his Will. He can cause Love, and show the Similitude of any person, and show the same by a Vision, let them be in what part of the

World they Will. He governeth 36 Legions of Spirits; and this is his Seal, which wear thou, etc.

(72.) ANDROMALIUS.-The Seventy-second Spirit in Order is named Andromalius. He is an Earl, Great and Mighty, appearing in the Form of a Man holding a Great Serpent in his Hand. His Office is to bring back both a Thief, and the Goods which be stolen; and to discover all Wickedness, and Underhand Dealing; and to punish all Thieves and other Wicked People and also to discover Treasures that be Hid. He ruleth over 36 Legions of Spirits. His Seal is this, the which wear thou as aforesaid, etc.

THESE be the 72 Mighty Kings and Princes which King Solomon Commanded into a Vessel of Brass, together with their Legions. Of whom BELIAL, BILETH, ASMODAY, and GAAP, were Chief. And it is to be noted that Solomon did this because of their pride, for he never declared other reason why he thus bound them. And when he had thus bound them up and sealed the Vessel, he by Divine Power did chase them all into a deep Lake or Hole in Babylon. And they of Babylon, wondering to see such a thing, they did then go wholly into the Lake, to break the Vessel open, expecting to find great store of Treasure therein. But when they had broken it open, out flew the Chief Spirits immediately, with their Legions following them; and they were all restored to their former places except BELIAL, who entered into a certain Image, and thence gave answers unto those who did offer Sacrifices unto him, and did worship the Image as their God, etc.

Observations

FIRST, thou shalt know and observe the Moon's Age for thy working. The best days be when the Moon Luna is 2, 4, 6, 8, 10, 12, or 14 days old, as Solomon saith; and no other days be profitable. The Seals of the 72 Kings are to be made in Metals. The Chief Kings' in Sol (Gold); Marquises' in Luna (Silver); Dukes' in Venus (Copper); Prelacies' in Jupiter (Tin); Knights' in Saturn (Lead) Presidents' in Mercury (Mercury); Earls' in Venus (Copper), and Luna (Silver), alike equal, etc. THESE 72 Kings be under the Power of AMAYMON, CORSON, ZIMIMAY or ZIMINAIR, and GÖAP, who are the Four Great Kings ruling in the Four Quarters, or Cardinal Points,[30] viz.: East, West, North, and South, and are not to be called forth except it be upon Great Occasions; but are to be Invocated and Commanded to send such or such a Spirit that is under their Power and Rule, as is shown in the following Invocations or Conjurations. And the Chief Kings may be bound from 9 till 12 o'clock at Noon, and from 3 till Sunset; Marquises may be bound from 3 in the afternoon till 9 at Night, and from 9 at Night till Sunrise; Dukes may be bound from Sunrise till Noonday in Clear Weather; Prelates may be bound any hour of the Day; Knights may

---

[30] These four Great Kings are usually called Oriens, or Uriens, Paymon or Paymonia, Ariton or Egyn, and Amaymon or Amaimon. By the Rabbins they are frequently entitled: Samael, Azazel, Azäel, and Mahazael.

from Dawning of Day till Sunrise, or from 4 o'clock till Sunset; Presidents may be bound any time, excepting Twilight, at Night, unless the King whom they are under be Invocated; and Counties or Earls any hour of the Day, so it be in Woods, or in any other places whither men resort not, or where no noise is, etc.

Classified List Of The 72 Chief Spirits Of The Goetia, According To Respective Rank.

(Seal in Gold.) KINGS.~(1.) Bael; (9.) Paimon; (13.) Beleth; (20.) Purson; (32.) Asmoday; (45.) Viné; (51.) Balam; (61.) Zagan; (68.) Belial.

(Seal in Copper.) DUKES.~(2.) Agares; (6.) Valefor; (8.) Barbatos; (11.) Gusion;(15.) Eligos; (16.) Zepar; (18.) Bathim; (19.) Sallos; (23.) Aim; (26.) Buné; (28.) Berith; (29.) Astaroth; (41.) Focalor; (42.) Vepar; (47.) Vual; (49.) Crocell; (52.) Alloces; (54.) Murmur; (56.) Gremory; (60.) Vapula; (64.) Haures; (67.) Amdusias; (71.) Dantalion.

(Seal in Tin.) PRINCES AND PRELATES.~(3.) Vassago; (12.) Sitri; (22.) Ipos; (33.) Gäap; (36.) Stolas; (55.) Orobas; (70.) Seere.

(Seal in Silver.) MARQUISES.~(4.) Samigina; (7.) Amon; (14.) Leraje; (24.) Naberius; (27.) Ronové; (30.) Forneus; (35.) Marchosias; (37.) Phenex; (43.) Sabnock; (44.) Shax; (59.) Orias; (63.) Andras; (65.) Andrealphus; (66.) Cimeies; (69.) Decarabia.

(Seal in Mercury.) PRESIDENTS.~ (5.) Marbas; (10.) Buer; (17.) Botis; (21.) Marax; (25.) Glasya-Labolas; (31.) Foras; (33.) Gäap; (39.) Malphas; (48.) Häagenti; (53.) Caim; (57.) Ose; (58.) Amy; (61.) Zagan; (62.) Valac.

(Seal in Copper and Silver alike equal.) EARLS, or COUNTS.~ (17.) Botis; (21.) Marax; (25.) Glasya-Labolas; (27.) Ronové; (34.)

Furfur; (38.) Halphas; (40.) Räum; (45.) Viné; (46.) Bifrons; (72.) Andromalius.

(Seal in Lead.) KNIGHTS.~(50.) Furcas.

NOTE.~It will be remarked that several among the above Spirits possess two titles of different ranks; e.g., (45.) Viné is both King and Earl; (25.) Glasya-Labolas is both President and Earl, etc. "Prince" and "Prelate" are apparently used as interchangeable terms. Probably the Seals of Earls should be made of Iron, and those of Presidents in mixture either of Copper and Silver, or of Silver and Mercury; as otherwise the Metal of one Planet, Mars, is excluded from the List; the Metals attributed to the Seven Planets being: to Saturn, Lead; to Jupiter, Tin; to Mars, Iron; to the Sun, Gold; to Venus, Copper; to Mercury, Mercury and mixtures of Metals, and to Luna, Silver.

IN a manuscript codex by Dr. Rudd, which is in the British Museum, Hebrew names of these 72 Spirits are given; but it appears to me that many are manifestly incorrect in orthography. The codex in question, though beautifully written, also contains many other errors, particularly in the Sigils. Such as they are, these names in the Hebrew of Dr. Rudd are here shown.

After the Hebrew of Dr. Rudd.

1 Beel	2 Agares	3 Vassago	4 Gamygir	5 Marbas	6 Valefon
בָאל	אגָאראש	ושאנו	גאמיגין	מארבש	ואלפטר
Figure 81	Figure 82	Figure 83	Figure 84.	Figure 85	Figure 86
7 Amon	8 Barbatos	9 Paimon	10 Buer	11 Gusion	12 Sitri
אמון	ברבטוש	פאימון	בואר	גוסיון	סיטרי
Figure 87	Figure 88	Figure 89	Figure 90	Figure 91	Figure 92
13 Beleth	14 Leraye	15 Eligos	16 Zepar	17 Botis	18 Bathin
כלאת	לריאך	אלינוש	זאפר	בוטיש	בָאתין
Figure 93	Figure 94	Figure 95	Figure 96	Figure 97	Figure 98
19 Sallos	20 Purson	21 Marax	22 Ipos	23 Aim	24 Naberius
שאלוש	פורשון	מאראם	יפוש	אים	נכריוש
Figure 99	Figure 100	Figure 101	Figure 102	Figure 103	Figure 104
Glass'Lablas	26 Bime	27 Ronove'	28 Berith	29 Astaroth	30 Forneus
גלאסיא־לב־ולש	בים	רונוו	ברית	אשטארות	פורנאוש
Figure 105	Figure 106	Figure 107	Figure 108	Figure 109	Figure 110
31 Foras	32 Asmoday	33 Gaap	34 Furfur	35 Marchosias	36 Stolas
פוראש	אסמורי	גאאף	פהורפהור	מרחוסיאש	שטולוש
Figure 111	Figure 112	Figure 113	Figure 114	Figure 115	Figure 116
37 Phenex	38 Malthas	39 Malphas	40 Raum	41 Focalor	42 Vepar
פאניס	מאלתש	מאלפש	ראום	פהוירכלור	ופאר
Figure 117	Figure 118	Figure 119	Figure 120	Figure 121	Figure 122
43 Sabnock	44 Shax	45 Vine'	46 Bifrons	47 Uvall	48 Haagenti
שבנוך	שאך	וינא	ביפהרונש	וואל	רָאגנטי
Figure 123	Figure 124	Figure 125	Figure 126	Figure 127	Figure 128
49 Crocell	50 Furcas	51 Balam	52 Alloces	53 Camio	54 Murmus
כרוכל	כהרכש	באלאם	אלוכאש	כאמיו	מורמוס
Figure 129	Figure 130	Figure 131	Figure 132	Figure 133	Figure 134
55 Orobas	56 Gmari	57 Voso	58 Avnas	59 Oriax	60 Naphula
ורובש	גמורי	ושו	אונש	וריאס	נפולא
Figure 135	Figure 136	Figure 137	Figure 138	Figure 139	Figure 140
61 Zagan	62 Valu	63 Andras	64 Haures	Andralphus	66 Kimaris
זאגאן	ואלו	אנדראש	דאוראש	אנדראלפה־וש	כימאריש
Figure 141	Figure 142	Figure 143	Figure 144	Figure 145	Figure 146
Amdukias	68 Belial	Decarabia	70 Seere	Dantalion	Andramelius
אמרוכיאש	בליאל	דכארכיא	שאר	דאנטאליון	אנדרומלי־וש
Figure 147	Figure 148	Figure 149	Figure 150	Figure 151	Figure 152

The Magical Circle

This is the Form of the Magical Circle of King Solomon, the which he made that he might preserve himself therein from the malice of these Evil Spirits. (See Frontispiece, Figure 153) This Magical Circle is to be made 9 feet across, and the Divine Names are to be written around it, beginning at EHYEH, and ending at LEVANAH, Luna.

(Colours.--The space between the outer and inner circles, where the serpent is coiled, with the Hebrew names written along his body, is bright deep yellow. The square in the centre of the circle, where the word "Master" is written, is filled in with red. All names and letters are in black. In the Hexagrams the outer triangles where the letters A, D, O, N, A, I, appear are filled in with bright yellow, the centres, where the T-shaped crosses are, blue or green. In the Penta-grams outside the circle, the outer triangles where "Te, tra, gram, ma, ton," is written, are filled in bright yellow, and the centres with the T crosses written therein are red.)[31]

---

[31] The coiled serpent is only shown in one private codex, the Hebrew names being in most cases simply written round in a somewhat spiral arrangement within the double circle. It is to be remembered that Hebrew is always written from right to left, p. 50 instead of from left to right like ordinary European languages. The small Maltese crosses are placed to mark the conclusion of each separate set of Hebrew names. These names are those of Deity Angels and Archangels allotted by the Qabalists to each of the 9 first Sephiroth or Divine Emanations. In English letters they run thus, beginning from the head of the serpent: ✠ Ehyeh Kether Metatron Chaioth Ha-Qadehs Rashith Ha-Galgalim S.P.M. (for "Sphere of the Primum Mobile") ✠ Iah Chokmah Ratziel Auphanim Masloth S.S.F (for "Sphere of the Fixed Stars," or S.Z. for "Sphere of the Zodiac") ✠ Iehovah Eolhim, Binah Tzadquiel Aralim Shab-bathai S. (for "Sphere") of Saturn ✠ El Chesed Tzadquiel Chaschmalim

The Magical Triangle Of Solomon

This is the Form of the Magical Triangle, into the which Solomon did command the Evil Spirits. It is to be made at 2 feet distance from the Magical Circle and it is 3 feet across. (See *Frontispiece Figure* 154.) Note that this triangle is to be placed toward that quarter whereunto the Spirit belongeth. And the base of the triangle is to be nearest unto the Circle, the apex pointing in the direction of the quarter of the Spirit. Observe thou also the Moon in thy working, as aforesaid, etc. Anaphaxeton is sometimes written Anepheneton.

(Colours.~Triangle outlined in black; name of Michael black on white ground; the three Names without the triangle written in red; circle in centre entirely filled in in dark green.)

Tzedeq S. of Jupiter ✠ Elohim Gibor Geburah Kamael Seraphim Madim S. of Mars ✠ Iehovah Eloah Va-Daäth Tiphereth Raphaêl Malakim Shemesh S. of the Sun ✠ Iehovah Tzabaoth Netzach Haniel Elohim Nogah S. of Venus. ✠ Elohim Tzabaoth Hod Michaêl Beni Elohim Kokav S. of Mercury ✠ Shaddaï El Chai Iesod Gabriel Cherubim Levanah S. of the Moon ✠.

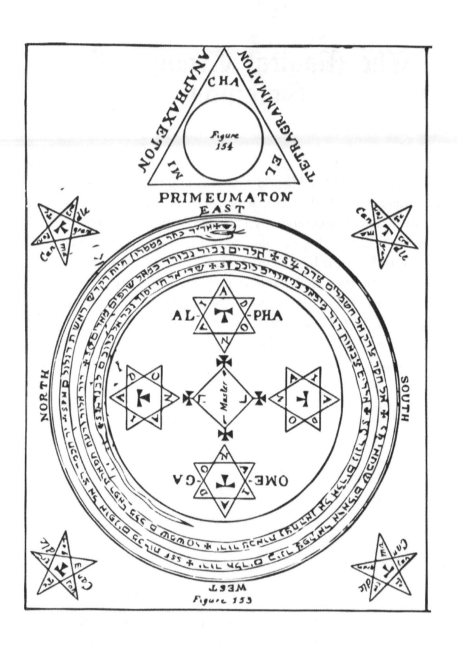

Figure 154

TETRAGRAMMATON
ANAPHAXETON
CHA
EL
MI

PRIMEUMATON
EAST

AL-PHA
OME-GA
Master

NORTH

SOUTH

WEST

Figure 153

The Hexagram Of Solomon

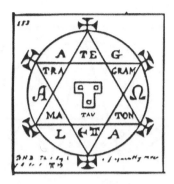

THIS is the Form of the Hexagram of Solomon, the figure whereof is to be made on parchment of a calf's skin, and worn at the skirt of thy white vestment, and covered with a cloth of fine linen white and pure, the which is to be shown unto the Spirits when they do appear, so that they be compelled to take human shape upon them and be obedient.

(Colours.--Circle, Hexagon, and T cross in centre outlined in black, Maltese crosses black; the five exterior triangles of the Hexagram where Te, tra, gram, ma, ton, is written, are filled in with bright yellow; the T cross in centre is red, with the three little squares therein in black. The lower exterior triangle, where the Sigil is drawn in black, is left white. The words "Tetragrammaton" and "Tau" are in black letters; and AGLA with Alpha and Omega in red letters.)

The Pentagram Of Solomon

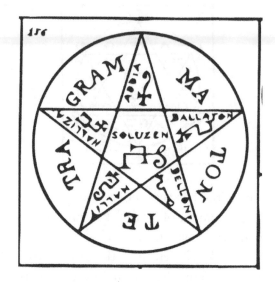

THIS is the Form of Pentagram of Solomon, the figure whereof is to be made in Sol or Luna (Gold or Silver), and worn upon thy breast; having the Seal of the Spirit required upon the other side thereof. It is to preserve thee from danger, and also to command the Spirits by.

(Colours.–Circle and pentagram outlined in black. Names and Sigils within Pentagram black also. "Tetragrammaton" in red letters. Ground of centre of Pentagram, where "Soluzen" is written, green. External angles of Pentagram where "Abdia", "Ballaton," "Halliza," etc., are written, blue.)

The Magic Ring Or Disc Of Solomon

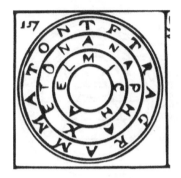

THIS is the Form of the Magic Ring, or rather Disc, of Solomon, the figure whereof is to be made in gold or silver. It is to be held before the face of the exorcist to preserve him from the stinking sulphurous fumes and flaming breath of the Evil Spirits.

(Colour.--Bright yellow. Letters, black.)

The Vessel Of Brass

THIS is the Form of the Vessel of Brass wherein King Solomon did shut up the Evil Spirits, etc. (See Figures 158 and 159 .) (Somewhat different forms are given in the various codices. The seal in Figure 160 was made in brass to cover this vessel with at the top. This history of the genii shut up in the brazen vessel by King Solomon recalls the story of "The Fisherman and the Jinni" in "The Arabian Nights." In this tale, however, there was only one jinni shut up in a vessel of yellow brass the which was covered at the top with a leaden seal. This jinni tells the fisherman that his name is Sakhr, or Sacar.)

(Colour.~Bronze. Letters.~Black on a red band.)

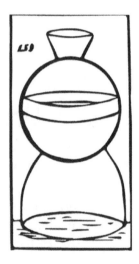

The Secret Seal Of Solomon.

THIS is the Form of the Secret Seal of Solomon, wherewith he did bind and seal up the aforesaid Spirits with their legions in the Vessel of Brass.

This seal is to be made by one that is clean both inwardly and outwardly, and that hath not defiled himself by any woman in the space of a month, but hath in prayer and fasting desired of God to forgive him all his sins, etc.

It is to be made on the day of Mars or Saturn (Tuesday or Saturday) at night at 12 o'clock, and written upon virgin parchment with the blood of a black cock that never trode hen. Note that on this night the moon must be increasing in light (i.e., going from new to full) and in the Zodiacal Sign of Virgo. And when the seal is so made thou shalt perfume it with alum, raisins dried in the sun, dates, cedar and lignum aloes.

Also, by this seal King Solomon did command all the aforesaid Spirits in the Vessel of Brass, and did seal it up with this same seal. He by it gained the love of all manner of persons, and overcame in battle, for neither weapons, nor fire, nor water could hurt him. And this privy seal was made to cover the vessel at the top withal, etc.

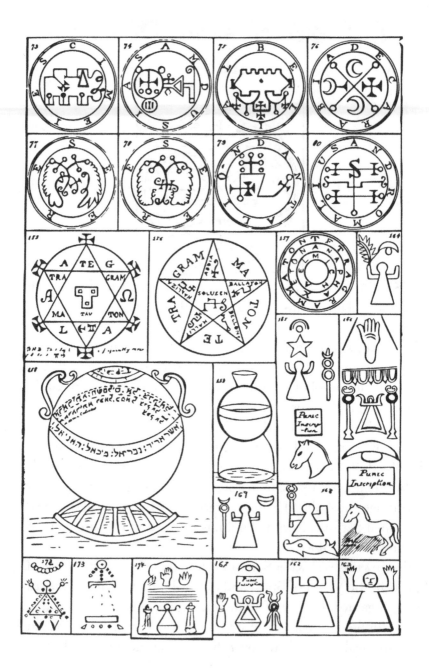

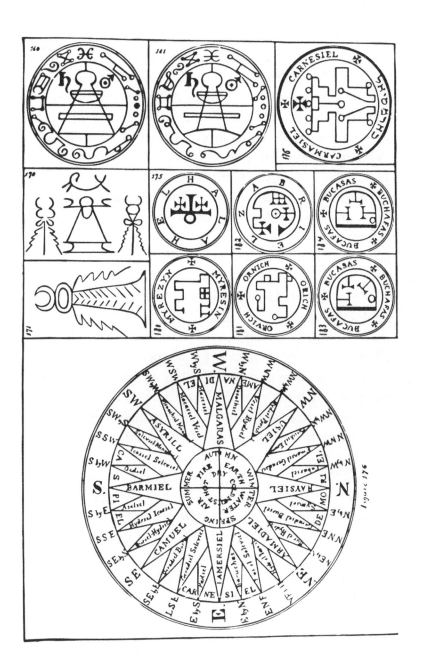

figure 176

Note: Figures 162 to 174 inclusive are interesting as showing a marked resemblance to the central design of the Secret Seal. It will be observed that the evident desire is to represent hieroglyphically a person raising his or her hands in adoration. Nearly all are stone sepulchral steles, and the execution of them is rough and primitive in the extreme. Most are in the Musée du Louvre at Paris.

Figures 162 and 163 are from the district of Constantine and show a figure raising its arms in adoration.

In Figure 164 , also from Constantine, the person bears a palm branch in the right hand. Above is a hieroglyphic representing either the Lunar Disc or the Sun in the heavens; but more probably the former.

Figure 165 is a more complicated stele. Above is the symbol already mentioned, then comes the sign of the Pentagram, represented by a five-pointed star, towards which the person raises his or her hands. Besides the latter is a rude form of caduceus. A brief inscription follows in the Punic character. The Punic or Carthaginian language is usually considered to have been a dialect. of Phœnician, and Carthage was of course a colony of Tyre. Beneath the Tunic inscription is a horse's head in better drawing than the sculpture of the rest of the stele, which would seem to imply that the rudeness of the representation of the human figure is intentional. This and the following stele are also from Constantine.

In Figure 166 again, the horse is best delineated by far. In addition to the other symbols there is either a hand or a foot, for it is almost impossible to distinguish which, at the head of the stele, followed by an egg-and-tongue moulding. The figure of the person with the arms raised is treated as a pure hieroglyphic and is placed between two rude caducei. The Lunar or Solar Symbol follows.

Figure 167 , also from Constantine, shows the last-mentioned symbol above. The figure with the arms raised is simply a hieroglyph, and is placed between an arm and hand on the one side, and a rude caduceus on the other.

Figure 168 shows the person holding a rude caduceus in the right hand, and standing above a dolphin. This latter, as in the case of the horse in 165 and 166, is by far the best delineated.

Figure 169 , this also being from Constantine, shows the usual human hieroglyph between a caduceus and a crescent.

Figure 170 is from the site of ancient Carthage. It is very rough in workmanship, and the designs are mere scratchings on the stone. The ensemble has the effect of an evil Sigil.

Figure 171 is also from Carthage and the various symbols appear to have become compressed into and synthesised in the form of a peculiarly evil-looking caduceus.

Figure 172 is from the decoration of a sepulchral urn found at Oldenburgh in Germany. It is remarkable as showing the same hieroglyphic human form with the crescent above; the latter in the Secret Seal of Solomon has a flattened top, and is therefore more like a bowl, and is placed across the hieroglyph.

Figure 173 is an Egyptian design which would show an analogy between the symbol and the idea of the force of the creation.

Figure 174 is a stele from Phœnicia somewhat similar to the others, except that the rudimentary caducei in Figures 166 and 170 are here replaced by two roughly drawn Ionic columns.

These last three designs are taken from the work of the Chevalier Emile Soldi-Colbert de Beaulieu, on the "Langue Sacrée."

In Figure 175 is given the Seal of the Spirit HALAHEL. This Spirit is said to be under the rule of BAEL, and to be of a mixed nature, partly good and partly evil, like the spirits of Theurgia-Goetia which follow in the second book of the Lemegeton.

The Other Magical Requisites

THE other magical requisites are: a sceptre, a sword, a mitre, a cap, a long white robe of linen, and other garments for the purpose;[32] also a girdle of lion's skin three inches broad, with all the names written about it which he round the outmost part of the Magical Circle. Also perfumes, and a chafing-dish of charcoal kindled to put the fumes on, to smoke or perfume the place appointed for action; also anointing oil to anoint thy temples and thine eyes with; and fair water to wash thyself in. And in so doing, thou shalt say as David said:

The Adoration At The Bath

"Thou shalt purge me with hyssop, O Lord! and I shall be clean: Thou shalt wash me, and I shall be whiter than snow."

And at the putting on of thy garments thou shalt say: THE ADORATION AT THE INDUING OF THE VESTMENTS.

"By the figurative mystery of these holy vestures (or of this holy vestment) I will clothe me with the armour of salvation in the strength of the Most High, ANCHOR; AMACOR; AMIDES; THEODINIAS; ANITOR; that my desired end may be effected through Thy strength, O ADONAI! unto Whom the praise and glory will for ever and ever belong! Amen!"

After thou hast so done, make prayers unto God according unto thy work, as Solomon hath commanded.

---

[32] In many Codices it is written "a sceptre or sword, a mitre or cap." By the "other garments" would be meant not only undergarments, but also mantles of different colours.

The Conjuration To Call Forth Any Of The Aforesaid Spirits.

I DO invoke and conjure thee, O Spirit, N.[33]; and being with power armed from the SUPREME MAJESTY, I do strongly command thee, by BERALANENSIS, BALDACHIENSIS, PAUMACHIA, and APOLOGIAE SEDES; by the most Powerful Princes, Genii, Liachidæ, and Ministers of the Tartarean Abode; and by the Chief Prince of the Seat of Apologia in the Ninth Legion, I do invoke thee, and by invoking conjure thee. And being armed with power from the SUPREME MAJESTY, I do strongly command thee, by Him Who spake and it was done, and unto whom all creatures be obedient. Also I, being made after the image of GOD, endued with power from GOD and created according unto His will, do exorcise thee by that most mighty and powerful name of GOD, EL, strong and wonderful; O thou Spirit N. And I command thee and Him who spake the Word and His FIAT was accomplished, and by all the names of God. Also by the names ADONAI, EL, ELOHIM, ELOHI, EHYEH, ASHER EHYEH, ZABAOTH, ELION, IAH, TETRAGRAMMATON, SHADDAI, LORD GOD MOST HIGH, I do exorcise thee and do powerfully command thee, O thou Spirit N., that thou dost forthwith appear unto me here before this Circle in a fair human shape, without any deformity or tortuosity. And by this ineffable name, TETRAGRAMMATON IEHOVAH, do I command thee, at the which being heard the elements are

---

[33] Here interpolate the name of the Spirit desired to be invoked. In some of the Codices there are faint variations in the form of wording of the conjurations, but not sufficient to change the sense, e. g., "Tartarean abode" for "Tartarean seat," etc.

overthrown, the air is shaken, the sea runneth back, the fire is quenched, the earth trembleth, and all the hosts of the celestials, terrestrials, and infernals, do tremble together, and are troubled and confounded. Wherefore come thou, O Spirit N., forthwith, and without delay, from any or all parts of the world wherever thou mayest be, and make rational answers unto all things that I shall demand of thee. Come thou peaceably, visibly, and affably, now, and without delay, manifesting that which I shall desire. For thou art conjured by the name of the LIVING and TRUE GOD, HELIOREN, wherefore fulfil thou my commands, and persist thou therein unto the end, and according unto mine interest, visibly and affably speaking unto me with a voice clear and intelligible without any ambiguity.

REPEAT this conjuration as often as thou pleasest, and if the Spirit come not yet, say as followeth:

The Second Conjuration.

I DO invoke, conjure, and command thee, O thou Spirit N., to appear and to show thyself visibly unto me before this Circle in fair and comely shape, without any deformity or tortuosity; by the name and in the name IAH and VAU, which Adam heard and spake; and by the name Of GOD, AGLA, which Lot heard and was saved with his family; and by the name IOTH, which Jacob heard from the angel wrestling with him, and was delivered from the hand of Esau his brother; and by the name ANAPHAXETON which Aaron heard and spake and was made wise; and by the name ZABAOTH, which Moses named and all the rivers were turned into blood; and by the name ASHER EHYEH ORISTON, which Moses named, and all the rivers brought forth frogs, and they ascended into the houses, destroying all things; and by the name ELION, which Moses named, and there was great hail such as had not been since the beginning of the world; and by the name ADONAI, which Moses named, and there came up locusts, which appeared upon the whole land, and devoured all which the hail had left; and by the name SCHEMA AMATHIA which Ioshua called upon, and the sun stayed his course; and by the name ALPHA and OMEGA, which Daniel named, and destroyed Bel, and slew the Dragon; and in the name EMMANUEL, which the three children, Shadrach, Meshach and Abed-nego, sang in the midst of the fiery furnace, and were delivered; and by the name HAGIOS; and by the SEAL[34] OF ADONI; and by ISCHYROS, ATHANATOS, PARACLETOS; and by O THEOS, ICTROS, ATHANATOS; and by these three secret names, AGLA, ON, TETRAGRAMMATON, do I adjure and constrain thee. And by these names, and by all the other names of the LIVING and TRUE GOD, the LORD ALMIGHTY, I do exorcise and command thee, O Spirit N., even by Him Who spake the Word and it was done, and to Whom all creatures are obedient; and by the dreadful judgments of GOD; and by the uncertain Sea of Glass, which is before the DIVINE MAJESTY, mighty and powerful; by the four beasts before the throne, having eyes before and behind; by the fire round about the throne; by the holy angels of Heaven; and by the mighty wisdom of GOD; I do potently exorcise thee, that thou appearest here before this Circle, to fulfil my will in all things which shall seem good unto me; by the Seal of BASDATHEA BAL-DACHIA; and by this name PRIMEUMATON, which Moses named, and the earth opened, and did swallow up Kora, Dathan, and Abiram. Wherefore thou shalt make faithful answers unto all my demands, O Spirit N., and shalt perform all my desires so far as in thine office thou art capable hereof. Wherefore, come thou, visibly, peaceably, and affably, now without delay, to manifest that

---

[34] In some "By the Seat of Adonai" or "By the Throne of Adonai." In these conjurations and elsewhere in the body of the text I have given the divine names correctly.

which I desire, speaking with a clear and perfect voice, intelligibly, and to mine understanding.

IF HE come not yet at the rehearsal of these two first conjurations (but without doubt he will), say on as followeth; it being a constraint:

The Constraint

I Do conjure thee, O thou Spirit N., by all the most glorious and efficacious names of the MOST GREAT AND INCOMPREHENSIBLE LORD GOD op HOSTS, that thou comest quickly and without delay from all parts and places of the earth and world wherever thou mayest be, to make rational answers unto my demands, and that visibly and affably, speaking with a voice intelligible unto mine understanding as aforesaid. I conjure and constrain thee, O thou Spirit N., by all the names aforesaid; and in addition by these seven great names wherewith Solomon the Wise bound thee and thy companions in a Vessel of Brass, ADONAI, PREYAI or PRERAI, TETRAGRAMMATON, ANAPHAXETON or ANEPHENETON, INESSENFATOAL or INESSENFATALL, PATHTUMON or PATHATUMON, and ITEMON; that thou appearest, here before this Circle to fulfil my will in all things that seem good unto me. And if thou be still so disobedient, and refusest still to come, I will in the power and by the power of the name of the SUPREME AND EVERLASTING LORD GOD WHO created both thee and me and all the world in six days, and what is contained therein, EIE, SARAYE, and by the power of this name PRIMEUMATON which commandeth the whole host of Heaven, curse thee, and deprive thee of thine office, joy, and place, and bind thee in the depths of the Bottomless Pit or Abyss, there to remain unto the Day of the Last Judgment. And I will bind thee in the Eternal Fire, and into the Lake of Flame and of Brimstone, unless thou comest quickly and appearest here before this Circle to do my will. Therefore, come thou! in and by the holy names ADONAI, ZABAOTH, ADONAI, AMIORAN. Come thou! for it is ADONAI who commandest thee.

IF THOU hast come thus far, and yet he appeareth not, thou mayest be sure that he is sent unto some other place by his King, and cannot come; and if it be so, invocate the King as here followeth, to send him. But if he do not come still, then thou mayest be sure that he is bound in chains in hell, and that he is not in the custody of his King. If so, and thou still hast a desire to call him even from thence, thou must rehearse the general curse which is called the Spirits' Chain.

Here followeth, therefore, the Invocation of the King:[35]

The Invocation Of The King

O THOU great, powerful, and mighty KING AMAIMON, who bearest rule by the power of the SUPREME GOD EL over all spirits both superior and inferior of the Infernal Orders in the Dominion of the East; I do invocate and command thee by the especial and true name Of GOD; and by that God that Thou Worshippest; and by the Seal of thy creation; and by the most mighty and powerful name Of GOD, IEHOVAH TETRAGRAMMATON who cast thee out of heaven with all other infernal spirits; and by all the most powerful and great names of GOD who created Heaven, and Earth, and Hell, and all things in them contained; and by their power and virtue; and by the name PRIMEUMATON who commandeth the whole host of Heaven; that thou mayest cause, enforce, and compel the Spirit N. to come unto me here before this Circle in a fair and comely shape, without harm unto me or unto any other creature, to

---

[35] It will depend on the quarter to which the Spirit is attributed, which of the four chief kings are to be invoked.

answer truly and faithfully unto all my requests; so that I may accomplish my will and desire in knowing or obtaining any matter or
thing which by office thou knowest is proper for him to perform or
accomplish, through the power of GOD, EL, Who created and doth
dispose of all things both celestial, aërial, terrestrial, and infernal.

AFTER thou shalt have invocated the King in this manner twice
or thrice over, then conjure the spirit thou wouldst call forth by the
aforesaid conjurations, rehearsing them several times together, and
he will come without doubt, if not at the first or second time of
rehearsing. But if he do not come, add the "Spirits' Chain" unto the
end of the aforesaid conjurations, and he will be forced to come,
even if he be bound in chains, for the chains must break off from
him, and he will be at liberty:

The General Curse, Called The Spirits' Chain, Against All Spirits That Rebel.

O THOU wicked and disobedient spirit N., because thou hast re-
belled, and hast not obeyed nor regarded my words which I have
rehearsed; they being all glorious and incomprehensible names of
the true GOD, the maker and creator of thee and of me, and of all
the world; I DO by the power of these names the which no creature
is able to resist, curse thee into the depth of the Bottomless Abyss,
there to remain unto the Day of Doom in chains, and in fire and
brimstone unquenchable, unless thou forthwith appear here before
this Circle, in this triangle to do my will. And, therefore, come thou
quickly and peaceably, in and by these names of GOD, ADONAI,
ZABAOTH, ADONAI, AMIORAN; come thou! come thou! for it
is the King of Kings, even ADONAI, who commandeth thee.

WHEN thou shalt have rehearsed thus far, but still be cometh not, then write thou his seal on parchment and put thou it into a strong black box;[36] with brimstone, assafœtida, and such like things that bear a stinking smell; and then bind the box up round with an iron wire, and bang it upon the point of thy sword, and hold it over the fire of charcoal; and say as followeth unto the fire first, it being placed toward that quarter whence the Spirit is to come:

The Conjuration Of The Fire

I CONJURE thee, O fire, by him who made thee and all other creatures for good in the world, that thou torment, burn, and consume this Spirit N., for everlasting. I condemn thee, thou Spirit N., because thou art disobedient and obeyest not my commandment, nor keepest the precepts of the LORD THY GOD, neither wilt thou obey me nor mine invocations, having thereby called thee forth, 1, who am the servant of the MOST HIGH AND IMPERIAL LORD GOD OF HOSTS, IEHOVAH, I who am dignified and fortified by His celestial power and permission, and yet thou comest not to answer these my propositions here made unto thee. For the which thine averseness and contempt thou art guilty of great disobedience and rebellion, and therefore shall I excommunicate thee, and destroy thy name and seal, the which I have enclosed in this box; and shall burn thee in the immortal fire and bury thee in immortal oblivion; unless thou immediately come and appear visibly and affably, friendly and courteously here unto me before this Circle, in this triangle, in a form comely and fair, and in no wise terrible, hurtful, or frightful to me or any other creature whatsoever upon the face of

---

[36] This BOX should evidently be in metal or in something which does not take fire easily.

earth. And thou shalt make rational answers unto my requests, and perform all my desires in all things, that I shall make unto thee.

AND if he come not even yet, thou shalt say as followeth:

The Greater Curse[37]

Now, O thou Spirit N., since thou art still pernicious and disobedient, and wilt not appear unto me to answer unto such things as I would have desired of thee, or would have been satisfied in; I do in the name, and by the power and dignity of the Omnipresent and Immortal Lord God of Hosts IEHOVAH TETRAGRAMMATON, the only creator of Heaven, and Earth, and Hell, and all that is therein, who is the marvellous Disposer of all things both visible and invisible, curse thee, and deprive thee of all thine office, joy, and place; and I do bind thee in the depths of the Bottomless Abyss there to remain until the Day of Judgment, I say into the Lake of Fire and Brimstone which is prepared for all rebellious, disobedient, obstinate, and pernicious spirits. Let all the company of Heaven curse thee! Let the sun, moon, and all the stars curse thee! Let the LIGHT and all the hosts of Heaven curse thee into the fire unquenchable, and into the torments unspeakable. And as thy name and seal contained in this box chained and bound up, shall be choken in sulphurous stinking substances, and burned in this material fire; so in the name IEHOVAH and by the power and dignity of these three names, TETRAGRAMMATON, ANAPHAXETON, and PRIMEUMATON, I do cast thee, O thou wicked and disobedient Spirit N., into the Lake of Fire which is prepared for the damnéd and accurséd spirits, and there to remain unto the day of doom, and never more to be remembered before the face of GOD,

---

[37] In some codices this is called "the Curse" only; but in one or two the "Spirits' Chain" is called "the Lesser Curse," and this the "Greater Curse."

who shall come to judge the quick, and the dead, and the world, by fire.

THEN the exorcist must put the box into the fire, and by-and-by the Spirit will come, but as soon as he is come, quench the fire that the box is in, and make a sweet perfume, and give him welcome and a kind entertainment, showing unto him the Pentacle that is at tile bottom of your vesture covered with a linen cloth, saying:

The Address Unto The Spirit Upon His Coming.

BEHOLD thy confusion if thou refusest to be obedient! Behold the Pentacle of Solomon which I have brought here before thy presence! Behold the person of the exorcist in the midst of the exorcism; him who is arméd by GOD and without fear; him who potently invocateth thee and calleth thee forth unto appearance; even him, thy master, who is called OCTINIMOS. Wherefore make rational answer unto my demands, and prepare to be obedient unto thy master in the name of the Lord:

BATHAL OR VATHAT RUSHING UPON ABRAC!

ABEOR COMING UPON ABERER.[38]

THEN he or they will be obedient, and bid thee ask what thou wilt, for he or they be subjected by God to fulfil our desires and commands. And when he or they shall have appeared and showed himself or themselves humble and meek, then shalt thou rehearse:

---

[38] In the Latin, "Bathal vel Vathat super Abrac ruens! Absor veniens super Aberer!"

The Welcome Unto The Spirit

WELCOME Spirit N., O most noble king[39] (or kings)! I say thou art welcome unto me, because I have called thee through Him who has created Heaven, and Earth, and Hell, and all that is in them contained, and because also thou hast obeyed. By that same power by the which I have called thee forth, I bind thee, that thou remain affably and visibly here before this Circle (or before this Circle and in this triangle) so constant and so long as I shall have occasion for thy presence; and not to depart without my license until thou hast duly and faithfully performed my will without any falsity.

THEN standing in the midst of the Circle, thou shall stretch forth thine hand in a gesture of command and say:

"BY TIME PENTACLE OF SOLOMON HAVE I CALLED THEE! GIVE UNTO ME A TRUE ANSWER."

Then let the exorcist state his desires and requests.

And when the evocation is finished thou shalt license the Spirit to depart thus:

The License To Depart

O THOU Spirit N., because thou hast-diligently answered unto my, demands, and hast been very ready and willing to come at my call, I do here license thee to depart unto thy proper place; without causing harm or danger unto man or beast. Depart, then, I say, and be thou very ready to come at my call, being duly exorcised and conjured by the sacred rites of magic. I charge thee to withdraw

---

[39] Or whatever his dignity may be.

peaceably and quietly, and the peace of GOD be ever continued between thee and me I AMEN!

AFTER thou hast given the Spirit license to depart, thou art not to go out of the circle until he or they be gone, and until thou shalt have made prayers and rendered thanks unto God for the great blessings He hath bestowed upon thee in granting thy desires, and delivering thee from all the malice of the enemy the devil.

Also note! Thou mayest command these spirits into the Vessel of Brass in the same manner as thou dost into the triangle, by saying: "that thou dost forthwith appear before this Circle, in this Vessel of Brass, in a fair and comely shape," etc., as hath been shown in the foregoing conjurations.

Explanation Of Certain Names Used In This Book Lemegeton

Eheie. Kether.--Almighty God, whose dwelling is in the highest Heavens:

Haioth.--The great King of Heaven, and of all the powers therein:

Methratton.--And of all the holy hosts of Angels and Archangels:

Reschith.--Hear the prayers of Thy servant who putteth his trust in Thee:

Hagalgalim.--Let thy Holy Angels be commanded to assist me at this time and at all times.

Iehovah.--God Almighty, God Omnipotent, hear my prayer:

Hadonat.--Command Thy Holy Angels above the fixed stars:

Ophanim.--To be assisting and aiding Thy servant:

Iophiel.~That I may command all spirits of air, water, fire, earth, and hell:

Masloth.~So that it may tend unto Thy glory and unto the good of man.

Iehovah.~God Almighty, God Omnipotent, hear my prayer:

Elohim.~God with us, God be always present with us.

Binah.~Strengthen us and support us, both now and for ever:

Aralim.~In these our undertakings, which we perform but as instruments in Thy hands:

Zabbathi (should be Shabbathii).~In the hands of Thee, the great God of Sabäoth.

Hesel (should be Chesed).~Thou great God, governor and creator of the planets, and of the Host of Heaven:

Hasmalim (should be Chashmalim).~Command them by Thine almighty power:

Zelez (should be Zedeq).~To be now present and assisting to us Thy poor servants, both now and for ever.

Elohim Geber (should be Gibor).~Most Almighty and eternal and ever living Lord God:

Seraphim.~Command Thy seraphim:

Camael, Madim.~To attend on us now at this time, to assist us, and to defend us from all perils and dangers.

Eloha.~O Almighty God! be present with us both now and for ever:

Tetragrammaton.~And let thine Almighty power and presence ever guard and protect us now and for ever:

Raphael.~Let thy holy angel Raphael wait upon us at this present and for ever:

Schemes (or Shemesh).~To assist us in these our undertakings.

Iehovah.~God Almighty, God Omnipotent, hear my prayer:

Sabäoth.~Thou great God of Sabäoth:

Netzah (or Netzach).~All-seeing God:

Elohim.~God be present with us, and let thy presence be now and always present with us:

Haniel.~Let thy holy angel Haniel come and minister unto us at this present.

Sabäoth.~O thou great God of Sabäoth, be present with us at this time and for ever:

Hodben (should be Hod simply).~Let Thine Almighty power defend us and protect us, both now and for ever:

Michael.~Let Michael, who is, under Thee, general of thy heavenly host:

Cochab.~Come and expel all evil and danger from us both now and for ever.

Sadai.~Thou great God of all wisdom and knowledge:

Jesal (should be Iesod).~Instruct Thy poor and most humble servant:

Cherubim.~By Thy holy cherubim:

Gabriel.~By Thy Holy Angel Gabriel, who is the Author and Messenger of good tidings:

Levanah.~Direct and support us at this present and for ever.

The Explanation Of The Two Triangles[40] In The Parchment

Alpha And Omega.~Thou, O great God, Who art the beginning and the end:

Tetragrammaton.~Thou God of Almighty power, be ever present with us to guard and protect us, and let Thy Holy Spirit and presence be now and always with us:

Soluzen.~I command thee, thou Spirit of whatsoever region thou art, to come unto this circle:

Halliza.~And appear in human shape:

Bellator (or Ballaton).~And speak unto us audibly in our mother-tongue:

Bellonoy (or Bellony).~And show, and discover unto us all treasure that thou knowest of, or that is in thy keeping, and deliver it unto us quietly:

Hallii. Hra.~And answer all such questions as we may demand without any defect now at this time.

An Explanation Of Solomon's Triangle

Anephezeton.~Thou great God of all the Heavenly Host:

Primeumaton.~Thou Who art the First and Last, let all spirits be subject unto us, and let the Spirit be bound in this triangle, which disturbs this place:

Michael.~By Thy Holy Angel Michael, until I shall discharge him.

---

[40] Evidently meaning both the Hexagram and the Pentagram of Solomon. (*See Figures* 155 *and* 156.)

(HERE ENDETH THIS FIRST BOOK OF THE LEMEGETON,
WHICH IS CALLED THE GOETIA.)

Conjurations

Preamble

Y^{se} Conjuratiouns of ye Books Goetia in ye Lemegeton which Solomoun ye Kynge did give unto Lemuel hys sonne rendered into ye Magicall or Angelike Language by our Illustrious and ever Glorious Frater, ye Wise Perdurabo, that Myghtye Chiefe of ye Rosy-Cross Fraternitye, now sepulchred in ye Vault of ye Collegium S.S. And soe may we doe alle!

Atte Ye Bathes Of Art

Asperges me, Domine, hyssopo, et mundabor:

Lavabis me, et super nivem dealbabor.

Atte Ye Induynge Of Ye Holy Vestures

In the mystery of these vestures of the Holy Ones, I gird up my power in the girdles of righteousness and truth in the power of the Most High: Ancor: Amacor: Amides: Theodonias: Anitor: let be mighty my power: let it endure for ever: in the power of Adonai, to whom the praise and the glory shall be; whose end cannot be.

Ye Fyrste Conjouratioun

I invoke and move thee, O thou, Spirit N.: and being exalted above ye in the power of the Most High, I say unto thee, Obey! in the name Beralensis, Baldachiensis, Paumachia, and Apologiae Sedes: and of the mighty ones who govern, spirits, Liachidae and ministers of the House of Death: and by the Chief Prince of the seat of Apologia in the Ninth Legion, I do invoke. thee and by invoking conjure thee. And being exalted above ye in the power of the, Most High., I say unto thee, Obey! in the name of him who spake and it was, to whom all creatures and things obey. Moreover I, whom God made in the likeness of God, who is the. creator according to his living breath, stir thee up in the name which is the voice of wonder of the mighty God, El, strong and unspeakable, O thou Spirit N.

And I say to thee obey, in the name of him who spake and it was; and in every one of ye, O ye names of God! Moreover in the names Adonai, El., Elohim., Elohi, Ehyeh Asher Ehyeh, Zabaoth, Elion, Iah, Tetragrammaton, Shaddai, Lord God Most High, I stir thee up; and in our strength I say Obey! O Spirit N. Appear unto His servants in a moment; before the circle in the likeness of a man; and visit me in peace. And in the ineffable name Tetragrammaton Iehovah, I say, Obey! whose mighty sound being exalted in power the pillars are divided, the winds of the firmament groan aloud; the fire burns not; the earth moves in earthquakes; and all things of the house of heaven and earth and the dwelling-place of darkness are as earthquakes, and are in torment, and are confounded in thunder. Come forth, O Spirit N. in. a moment: let thy dwelling-place be empty, apply unto us the secrets of Truth and obey my power. Come forth, visit us in peace, appear unto my eyes; be friendly: Obey the living breath! For I stir thee up in the name of the God of Truth who liveth for ever, Helioren. Obey the living breath, therefore continually unto the end as my thoughts appear to my eyes: therefore be friendly: speaking the secrets of Truth in voice and in understanding.

De Secounde Conjouratioun

I invoke thee, and move thee, and stir thee up O Spirit N. appear unto my eyes before the circle in the likeness of a man in the names and by the name Iah and Vau, which Adam spake and in the name of God, Agla, which Lot spake: and it was as pleasant deliverers unto him and his house and in the name Ioth which Iacob spake in the voice of the Holy ones who cast him down, and it was also as pleasant deliverers in the anger of his brother and in the name

Anaphaxeton, which Aaron spake and it was as the Secret Wisdom and in the name Zabaoth which Mosheh spake, and all things of water were as blood; and in the name Asher Ehyeh Oriston, which Mosheh spake, and all waters were bringing forth creatures who wax strong, which lifted up unto the houses, which destroy all things and in the name of Elion which Mosheh spake, and it was as stones from the firmament of wrath, such as was not in the ages of Time the beginning of the Earth and in the name of Adni, which Mosheh spake and there appeared creatures of earth who destroyed what the big stones did not: and in the name Schema Amathia, which Ioshua invoked, and the Sun remained over ye, O ye hills the seats of Gibeon, and in the names Alpha and Omega which Daniel spake, and destroyed Bel and the Dragon: and in the name Emmanuel which the sons of God sang praises in the midst of the burning plain, and flourished in conquest: and in the name Hagios, and by the Throne of Adni, and in Ischyros, Athanatos, Paracletos: and in O Theos, Ictros, Athanatos. And in these names of secret truth, Agla, On, Tetragrammaton, do I invoke and move thee. And in these names, and all things that are the names of the God of Secret Truth who liveth for ever, the All-Powerful. I invoke and stir thee up, O spirit N. Even by him who spake it was, to whom all creatures are obedient and in the Extreme Justice and Anger of God; and by the veil(?) that is before the glory of God, mighty; and by the creatures of living breath before the Throne whose eyes are east and west; by the fire in the fire of just Glory of the Throne; by the Holy ones of Heaven; and by the secret wisdom of God, I, exalted in power, stir thee up. Appear before this circle; obey in all things that I say; in the seal Basdathea Baldachia; and in this Name Primeumaton, which Mosheh spake, and the earth was divided, and Korah, Dathan, and Abiram fell in the depth. Therefore obey in all things, O spirit N., obey thy creation. Come thou forth: appear unto my eyes; visit us in peace, be friendly; come forth in the 24th of a moment; obey my power, speaking the secrets of Truth in voice and in understanding!

Ꝑe Constraynte

I stir thee up, O spirit N. in all things that are the names of glory and power of God the Great One who is greater than understanding, Adni Ihvh Tzabaoth, come forth in the 24th of a moment, let Thy dwelling-place be empty; apply thyself unto the secret truth and obey my power: appear unto my eyes, visit us in peace, speaking the secrets of truth in voice and understanding. I stir thee up and move thee, O spirit N., in all the names that I have said, and I add these one and six names wherein Solomon, the lord of the secret wisdom, placed yourselves, spirits of wrath, in a vessel, Adonai,. Preyai Tetra-grammaton, Anaphaxeton Inessenfatoal, Pathtomon and Itemon: appear before this circle; obey in all things my power. And as thou art he that obeys not and comes not I shall be in thy power, O God Most High that liveth for ever, who is the creator of all things in six days Eie, Saraye, and in my power in the name Prieumaton that ruleth over the palaces of heaven, Curse Thee, and destroy thy seat, joy, and power; and I bind thee in the depth of Abaddon, to remain until the day of judgment whose end cannot be. And I bind thee in the fire of sulphur mingled with poison and the seas of fire and sulphur: come, forth, therefore, obey my power and appear before, this circle. Therefore come forth in the name of the Holy Ones Zabaoth, Adonai, Amioran. Come! for I am Adonai who stir thee up.

Ꝑe Potent Invocatioun Of Ꝏys Kynge

O thou great powerful governor Amaimon, who reigneth exalted in the power of the only El above all spirits in the kingdoms of the East, (South, West, North), I invoke and move thee in the name of the true God, and in God whom thou worshippest: and in the, seal of thy creation: and in the mighty names of God, Iehevohe Tetra-grammaton, who cast thee down from Heaven, thou and the spirits of darkness, and in all the names of the mighty God who is the creator of Heaven and earth, and the dwelling of darkness, and all things and in their power and brightness; and in the name Primeumaton who reigns over the palaces of Heaven. Bring forth, I say, the spirit N.; bring him forth in the 24th of a moment let his dwelling be, empty until he visits us in peace, speaking the secrets of truth; until he obey my power and his creation in the power of God, El, who is the Creator and doth dispose of all things, heaven, firmament, earth, and the dwelling of darkness.

Þe Generall Curse.
Þelept Þe Spirits' Chayne, Against All Spirits Þt Rebelle

O thou wicket spirit N. that obeyeth not, because I made a law and invoked the names of the glorious and ineffable God of Truth, the creator of all, and thou obeyest not the mighty sounds that I make: therefore I curse thee in the depth of Abaddon to remain until the day of judgment in torment in fire and in sulphur without end, until thou appear before our will and obey my power. Come, therefore, in the 24th of a moment, before the circle in the triangle in this name and by this name of God, Adni, Tzabaoth, Adonai, Amioran. Come! Come! for it is the Lord of Lords Adni, that stirreth thee up.

Þe Conjouratioun Of Þe Fyre

I stir thee up, O thou fire, in him who is thy Creator and of all creatures. Torment, burn, destroy the spirit N. always whose end cannot be, I judge thee in judgment and in extreme justice, O spirit N., because thou art he that obeyeth not my power and obeyeth not that law which the Lord God made, and obeyeth not the Mighty Sounds and the Living Breath which I invoke, which I send: Come forth, I, who am the Servant of the game Most High governor Lord God powerful, Iehovohe, I who am exalted in power and am mighty in his power above ye, O thou who comest not giving obedience and faith to him that liveth and triumpheth. Therefore I say the judgment: I curse thee and destroy the name N. and the seal N., which I have placed in this dwelling of poison, and I burn thee in fire whose end cannot be; and I cast thee down unto the seas of torment, out of which thou shalt not rise until thou come to my eyes: visit me in peace: be friendly before the circle in the $\triangle$ in the 24th of a moment in the likeness of a man not unto the terror of the sons of men the creatures or all things on the face of the earth. Obey my power like reasoning creatures; obey the living breath, the law which I speak.

Ye Greter Curse

Hearken to me, O ye Heavens! O thou Spirit N. because thou art the disobedient one who is wicked and appearest not, speaking the secrets of truth according to the, living breath; I, exalted in the power of God, the All powerful, the center of the circle, powerful God who liveth, whose end cannot be., Iehevohe Tetragrammaton,, the only creator of heaven, earth, and dwelling of darkness and, all that is in their palaces; who disposeth in secret wisdom of all things in darkness and light: Curse thee and cast thee down and destroy thy seat, joy and power, and I bind thee in the depths of Abaddon, to remain until the day of judgment whose end cannot be, I say, unto the seas of fire and sulphur which I have prepared for the wicked spirits that obey not; the sons of iniquity.

Let the company of heaven curse thee!

Let the sun, moon, all the stars curse thee!

Let the light and all the Holy Ones of Heaven curse thee unto the burning flame that liveth for ever, and unto the torment unspeakable!

And even as thy name and seal, which I have put in this dwelling of poison, shall be in torment among creatures of sulphur and bitter sting, burning in fire of earth, in them Iehevohe and exalted in power in these three names, Tetragrammaton Anaphaxeton, Primeumaton, I cast thee down, O wicked spirit N. unto the seas of fire and sulphur which are prepared for the wicked spirits that obey not, the sons of iniquity, to remain until the day of judgment; let the Mercies of God forget thee; let the face of God forget the face of N. who will not see light: let God forget, I say that shall be the balance of justice over the sons of living breath and death and the world, by fire.

Ye Addresse Unto Ye Spirit On Hys Coming

Behold! I confound thee as thou art he that obeys not! Behold the mysteries of the seal of Solomon which I bring forth unto thy power and presence! Behold the creator, the centre of the circle of the living breath; he that is exalted in the power of God and shall not see unto the terror: he that powerfully invoketh and stirreth thee up unto visible appearance: he, the lord of thy governments whose Name is called Octinomos.

Obey, therefore, my power as a reasoning creature -in the name of the Lord.

Ye Welcome Unto Yᵉ Spirit Dygnytie

I am he that is looking with gladness upon thee, O thou spirit . . . N. beautiful and praiseworthy! with gladness I say, because thou art called in him who is creator of Heaven and earth and the dwelling of darkness, and all things that are in their palaces, and because thou art the servant of obedience. In these the power by which thou art obedient to the living breath, I bind thee to remain visible to our eyes in power and presence as the servant of fealty before the circle until I say "Descend unto thy dwelling" until the living breath of the voice of the Lord is according to the law which shall be given unto thee.

By the seal of the secret wisdom of Solomon thou art called!
Obey the mighty sounds! obey the living breath of the voice of the Lord!

Follows ye charge.

𝔜𝔢 𝔏𝔦𝔠𝔢𝔫𝔰𝔢 𝔗𝔬 𝔜𝔢 𝔖𝔭𝔦𝔯𝔦𝔱 𝔜ᵗ 𝔥𝔢 𝔐𝔞𝔶𝔢 𝔇𝔢𝔭𝔞𝔯𝔱

O thou Spirit N. because thou art the servant of fealty and obedience, and because thou art he that obeyeth my power and thy creation; therefore I say Descend unto thy dwelling, obey the law which I have made, without terror to the sons of men, creatures, all things upon the surface of the earth.

Descend therefore I say, and be thou as stewards of Time; come forth in a moment, even as servants that hearken to the voice of the Lord; in the moment in which I invoke thee and stir thee up and move thee in the, mysteries of the secret wisdom of the Creator!

Descend unto thy dwelling place in pleasure: let there be the mercies of God upon thee: be friendly in continuing; whose long continuance shall be comforters unto all creatures. Amen.

Contents

Made in the USA
Coppell, TX
11 January 2025

44243814R00062

The Lesser Key of Solomon, also known as Salomonis Regis or Lemegeton, is an anonymous grimoire on demonology. It was compiled in the mid-17th century, mostly from materials a couple of centuries older.

ISBN 9798722396952

90000

9 798722 396952

STREAMS *of* LIGHT
from a HEART BROKEN

HOPEFUL REFLECTIONS ON A
GRIEF-SHADOWED JOURNEY

JULIE GRANT